LIVE LIKE A STARTUP

TAKE THE INITIATIVE AND TRANSFORM YOUR LIFE

YANIV RIVLIN

Producer & International Distributor
eBookPro Publishing
www.ebook-pro.com

LIVE LIKE A STARTUP
Yaniv Rivlin

Copyright © 2023 Yaniv Rivlin

All rights reserved; no parts of this book may be reproduced
or transmitted in any form or by any means, electronic
or mechanical, including photocopying, recording, taping,
or by any information retrieval system, without the
permission, in writing, of the author.

Translation: Noam Heller
Editing: Mathew Berman
Contact: Yanivrivlin1@gmail.com

ISBN 9798858790525

THIS BOOK IS DEDICATED

To the loving memory of my father, Mark Rivlin (1951-2023), who passed away suddenly as this book was in the process of being published in English. Daddy, the nobility of your soul, wisdom, humility, and infinite kindness will be cherished in my heart forever. You had a profound impact on my life and this book wouldn't have been possible without you.

CONTENTS

Just Do It. The Rest Will Follow..7

CHAPTER 1
The Golan Heights... 11
A Word to the Wise by *NUSEIR YASSIN*
(Nas Daily), renowned vlogger 25
A Word to the Wise by NETA RIVKIN,
Israeli rhythmic gymnast 27

CHAPTER 2
Between Lebanon and Malibu... 30
My Word to the Wise 46
A Word to the Wise by *STAV SHAFFIR*,
former Israeli politician and founder of the
"Shira Center" – an academic institute for
people with special needs 47

CHAPTER 3
Jerusalem, the Hebrew University......................................51
My Word to the Wise 74
A Word to the Wise from *TOMER AVITAL*,
an Independent Journalist..75

CHAPTER 4
A Mansion in Canada 79
My Word to the Wise 102
A Word to the Wise from *LANA ZAHER*,
Partner at "Al-Arz" Tahini 103

CHAPTER 5
Harvard 106
My Word to the Wise 133
A Word to the Wise by **TOMER COHEN**,
CEO of BUYME 134

CHAPTER 6
Atlanta..137
My Word to the Wise 166
A Word to the Wise by **DORON MEDALIE**,
Musician, Composer, Artistic Director.................................... 167

CHAPTER 7
Tel Aviv... 170
My Word to the Wise 188
A Word to the Wise by **NARKIS ALON**,
Social Entrepreneur 189

CHAPTER 8
Between Silicon Valley and Ben-Gurion Boulevard 193
My Word to the Wise 207
A Word to the Wise from **OFIR CHARLAP RIVLIN**,
Impact and Innovation Entrepreneur in Real Estate 208

CHAPTER 9
From a Bird's Eye View 212
My Word to the Wise 239
A Word to the Wise from **ADI ALTSCHULER**,
Founder of "Krembo Wings" and "Zikaron Basalon" 240

CHAPTER 10
Between Midburn and Times Square............................. 244

Just Do It. The Rest Will Follow

OMER ZERAHIA, entrepreneur and academic in the field of cannabis, founder of MSCIS, Yaniv's friend from the Hebrew University

*If you want something done,
give it to the busiest guy in the room.*

Yaniv's idea was born on a morning he and I went out for a run. This was after my company went public, and just before Yaniv's went public on the New York Stock Exchange. We talked, as always, about friends, business, and current events. During our conversation, Yaniv, who came from the world of philanthropy (as you will read in this book), raised the topic of having people from our social circle contribute to society; people who make and will continue to make a lot of money beyond their paychecks, i.e., from stock and options.

"How is there no platform that lets us donate from our current and future wealth to social causes? And anyway, why aren't we all philanthropists!?"

"What are you proposing?" I asked.

"To form a fund that would do it for us," he replied,

"one that will amalgamate a certain percentage of our equity and donate it to causes we all agree are worthy."

"Great idea, but…who's going to do it? Just a reminder, we're both super busy. I mean, you're planning a wedding, writing a book, helping out companies and organizations, and mainly playing a significant role in a global company that is just about to have its IPO in New York…"

"Well, who if not us?" Yaniv asked and smiled. It reminded me of the sentence that has stuck with us since graduate school, when we first met: "If you want something done, give it to the busiest guy in the room."

That is how "1point8" came to be. Apart from what it does, it was founded by people who are doers themselves.

***

Ever since I can remember, I've been busy with something. It hasn't always turned out well, but at least I was doing something, moving forward.

I've learned that taking action brings with it more action. Similar to relationships – when you're spoken for, you suddenly feel like the most desired person in the room. The same goes for taking action. When you act, additional offers start coming your way.

For many of us, our initial response to such offers is rejection. "I'm terribly busy," "I don't want to half-ass this, "I want to give it my all," "I want to focus on one project at a time." Similar to how we treat relationships.

But, come to think of it, why? Activity, among other things, moves along the efficiency axis. We feel this particularly when juggling several projects, and time is short. Suddenly, we become way more efficient and capable of taking on more than expected. How does this happen to us, particularly when we're overloaded with work? Is this due to stress (which isn't necessarily positive)? Is there another way we can become more efficient and simply accomplish more?

I believe there is, and it has to do with our level of excitement about what we're doing. All of us can find the time, no matter how busy we are, for what excites us: friends, family, trips, food... Excitement is the catalyst of action. Excitement boosts our motivation, and motivation makes us more efficient, and efficiency helps us get more done.

In Yaniv's book, you'll read about taking action and, between the lines, you'll be able to identify tremendous excitement, which continues to breed more action.

So, get excited and do stuff, it doesn't matter what, just do it. The rest will follow.

CHAPTER 1

The Golan Heights
Green Meadows and Running Rivers

We gathered in Times Square, New York, at four in the afternoon. The plaza, glistening with the same tempting quality that lured me in as a child, flickered its promises on billboards for people passing by to see. We lifted our gaze to the sign that read "BIRD," a light blue tinge glowing across one of the buildings. Thoughts raced through my mind: How did I, a small-town kid from the north of Israel, whose dreams didn't extend beyond the local river, manage to become a senior executive of an international company that was now revolutionizing the world?

Like the illuminated letters flickering on the sign, my memory flooded with a flux of flashing images, pivotal moments that had led me to this point in life: my early days as a student, strenuously juggling work and school, the inspiring time spent in Canada with promising youth from around the world, the two, insightful years I'd spent at Harvard (practically pinching myself each day to ensure it wasn't a dream), life in distant Atlanta arranging journeys to Israel for influencers, and finally, standing in the middle of Tel Aviv's bustling avenues and realizing that shared electric scooters were tailor-made for this city.

Among those flashing memories were moments of hardships and failure – moments of weary desperation trying to sell cosmetics in a Canadian mall, and sighs of disappointment shuffling through numerous letters of rejection. Those moments were no less central to my progress and serve as a humbling reminder of the fragility of success.

***

Nothing about my childhood could have predicted the triumphs that lay ahead. I wasn't born with a silver spoon in my mouth, nor was I surrounded by people with far-reaching dreams. I didn't stand out, nor did I excel. I was an average student with average grades, nothing more. My childhood dream – which I had absolutely no chance of fulfilling – was to be Michael Jordan. Another dream of mine (significantly more realistic) was spending Saturdays with friends relaxing by the local river, the most exciting thing imaginable at the time.

To put things more accurately: my starting point in life was behind the curve. I was born in April of 1982, 34 weeks into my mother's pregnancy. As a premature baby weighing 4.6 pounds, my life was at risk, and my parents had to endure long and taxing weeks of uncertainty. Finally, when I reached the three-month mark at a healthy weight of 6.6 pounds, they let out a celebratory sigh of relief.

Two months after my birth, the First Lebanon War erupted. Apart from the challenges of handling a newborn, my mom spent agonizing nights worrying about my dad, who was in the crossfire as a reservist for the Israeli Defense Forces in Lebanon. Rockets flew incessantly above our house, and one of them actually landed on our doorstep.

Our house was located in a small kibbutz (a communal living arrangement popular in Israel) in the north of Israel, a remote area where both my parents, brimming with ideology and values, came as volunteers. My mom, Sima, flew in from Canada, and my dad, Mark, from the United States. A pair of young hippies, they left behind their convenient lives to fulfill their Zionist dream in a novel, socialist kibbutz. The first four years of my life were spent in that utopian setting, running barefoot from the communal children's home to the grassy fields. The few, hazy memories I have of that time include my Canadian grandparents, Esther and Lionel, flying in from Montreal with a bag full of clothes, identical articles for every kid in my grade. A gift solely for their grandson, was, of course, out of the question.

Life on the kibbutz was pleasantly simple. My dad spent his days rushing from the dairy farm to the factory, and my mom taught English at the local school. For better or worse, living with foreign parents meant that I developed my own language – "Heblish" – an endearing, childish blend of English and Hebrew.

Growing up, I was a smart, curious kid who wanted to know it all. By the age of four, and thanks to my impressive collection of toy cars, I had taught myself to read English. Eager to know where each car was manufactured, I learned to read the countries engraved on the back. Gradually, my interest in sports grew, and I began ravenously devouring the sports column in The Jerusalem Post newspaper we had lying around the house.

The decision to fly to Montreal came after my parents grew increasingly disillusioned with the kibbutz and chose to take my younger sister and me halfway across the world to start anew. In Montreal, my mom decided to get me evaluated, and after a series of intelligence tests, the assessor tagged me as a moderately gifted child with an IQ of 140.

There were a few reasons for their disappointment. For one, I was often sick as a toddler, and the kibbutz didn't quite know how to handle my condition. Whenever I vomited during pre-school hours, they would ignorantly force me to eat again. But my parents didn't give up. Adamant to find the reason for their child's gaunt appearance and tenacious sickness, they ran from one doctor to the next, but couldn't find a satisfying answer. Incidentally, it was a hospital intern who ended up finding the root of my problem – a rare ear infection. A special device was inserted into my ears, and finally, at the age of three, I was able to stand on my own two feet.

On the whole, my mom wasn't happy with the kibbutz's education system (the fact that my drawings were all in black surely didn't help). But sadly, there wasn't much room for change – my teacher was the head of the kibbutz's education department, so there wasn't really anyone else to approach on the matter.

While my parent's utopian dream of living on a kibbutz had been shattered, their Zionist dream lingered on. Sima and Mark were determined to live in Israel, and in order to gather their thoughts and plan out their next steps, they moved the family to Canada for a year where we lived with my grandparents. It was a time of significant bonding and one where I gained my first, insightful perspective on life abroad. I forgot my Hebrew and perfected my English, explored large museums and parks, and even celebrated my birthday at McDonald's with Ronald McDonald, a drunk clown my parents had hired.

Ultimately, we returned to Katzrin, a sleepy town located on the Golan Heights, where my parents live to this day. At the time, Katzrin was comprised of a mere 2,000 citizens, a tight-knit community of people who knew each other well. Over the years, Katzrin has welcomed additional residents, but as is customary of peripheral areas, many came from poor socio-economic backgrounds. Nowadays, even though the population size has grown, it is still a humble 8,000 residents.

***

Returning to Israel after a year in Montreal was confusing. At five years old, I had forgotten most of my Hebrew. Frustration built up inside whenever I couldn't properly express myself, like the time I struggled to find the Hebrew word for "bin," and drove my kindergarten teacher crazy in an attempt to get her to understand. I was completely unaware of the tacit semantic rules and would often get into trouble for putting together sentences that came off as rude.

As both Hebrew and English weren't taught to me properly, the confusion surrounding languages haunts me to this day. At school, they put me in an English-speaking class and gave me a free pass on grammar lessons because they believed I was fluent. Later in life, when I tried to get into Harvard, I failed the Toefl test – an entry exam meant to assess one's competence in the English language. It was a mistake to overlook the basic rules of English, and possibly the reason I find it difficult to acquire new languages as an adult.

In the first grade, I was diagnosed with dysgraphia, a writing impairment inherited from my mom. My parents turned down my teacher's recommendation to copy bits of newspaper articles to improve my handwriting, and instead, sent me to an occupational therapist. That same teacher, by the way, phoned my parents one day to complain that I'd pointed out a mistake she had made in front of the whole class.

In third grade, my school handed out a test meant to spot gifted kids. While my score wasn't enough to pass as qualified, the test I'd done back in Montreal came in handy, and my mom managed to land me a spot in a special educational program for gifted kids. In fact, she taught there and later even became the principal.

Each Tuesday, along with my childhood friend Yaron Meirovitch – who is, compared to me, an actual genius, and currently pursuing his post-doctorate in neuroscience at MIT – I was taken to Tel-Hai campus, which had an education center for gifted youth. The drive there was full of winding roads swerving along the mountain, and memories of those rides include Yaron's incessant car sickness, but even worse, the lingering feelings of angst and dread. I didn't feel worthy of my place in that group of talented kids. My mom had secured my spot, I thought, and the notion of having to prove myself was paralyzing.

But the anxiety was well worth it, because what we learned there was fascinating – the topics ranged from medicine to robotics, animation, and chess (my biggest accomplishment was securing a draw against Yaron – what an achievement!). In retrospect, being one of the highest-achieving students in the group, I never felt like I deserved to be there.

Likewise, my teachers never expected anything great out of me. My grades weren't very high, and I made sure to hide every test I failed from my parents, especially my mom. If they managed to find out, they would shake their heads in disappointment, and rightfully so. Hebrew lessons were challenging, and so was math, even though I'm actually quite good when it comes to certain aspects of it. I can run complex calculations in my head, and solve them intuitively, but without being able to explain what I did. A different teaching method was needed for me to thrive. On the whole, I believe that something is undoubtedly wrong with the current system, which is evidently failing to prepare students for adulthood.

For most of my life, my handwriting was horrible and full of typos. But things became a bit easier after I was diagnosed with ADHD and dysgraphia, granting me classroom accommodations like extra time on tests or reading questions out loud. It's important to note that learning disability assessments weren't as popular back then as they are today. I was one of only two kids in my whole grade with that diagnosis.

In seventh grade, I moved to the area's regional school, which would later become home to one of the greatest murder mysteries to shock Israel – the murder of a 13-year girl named Tair Rada, who was found dead in the school's bathroom stall. Her brother, Roy, was in my grade.

Longing for something else, my interest then shifted to the humanistic side of the pendulum, as I was exposed to sociology for the first time (I was one of five boys in the class). I remember admiring the teacher's teaching method - the way he dictated the material to us - and wondering why the others weren't doing the same.

As for after-school hours, my sister and I were often left on our own to heat up refrigerated food as our parents spent full days at work. My dad worked at a factory, then moved on to Intel, where he did shifts including four days of work, four days of rest. When Intel had to lay off some employees, he got into tourism, and today, he works as a driver and is the landlord of an additional apartment on the second floor of the family house. Apart from his career, my dad is an absolute genius when it comes to general knowledge, and even made an appearance on the Israeli version of "The Weakest Link" (You are the weakest link, goodbye!). My mom continued walking the path of education and taught

English to college students, in addition to her job as a school principal.

Their ambitiousness left a mark on me, and in retrospect, I know I owe them a lot for the values and work ethic they instilled in me. If my mom was the one who pushed me forward, my dad was the one who taught me the joys of a relaxing morning ritual – newspaper and coffee in the comfort of my bed.

As I grew older, my curiosity evolved from the origins of toy cars to politics. I knew everything, including the number of mandates each political party had ever received. I read the paper, front to back, and never once missed the news flickering on our TV each evening. In the '90s, when talk surfaced of withdrawing from the Golan Heights as part of a peace treaty with Syria, I agreed with the idea, even though I, myself, lived in the area. And when then-prime minister Yitzhak Rabin delivered a speech in my hometown, I wholeheartedly stood behind him.

I'm still obsessed with politics, but my general knowledge in the field has certainly declined, probably due to Google's impeccable ability to give us all the answers with a click of a button.

I wasn't very popular growing up, but I wasn't unpopular either. A fairly low level of self-esteem loomed over me, at least until I reached Harvard. When it came to girls, the first relationship I had was in the army. I found it hard to believe that girls could be into me, so much so, that in the 9th grade, when a girl named Maria asked me if I wanted to be her boyfriend, I refused. She couldn't possibly want a guy like me. One nickname my friends used to dub me was "pompom nose," not to mention my big ears, which also served as great joke material. If I could talk to the kid I was back then, I'd tell him not to be so hard on himself. Appreciate who you are, I'd say.

Despite my frail self-image, I wasn't lonely. I had groups of friends piling into my house each day to play new games I owned from overseas. Sports games were my favorite, including "NBA 1" for the PC, with graphics so bad you could barely recognize the players. Championship Manager was another favorite of mine, and through which I vicariously lived out my dream of being a soccer coach.

In high school, my grades weren't all too impressive, despite studying hard for the matriculation exams. I tried with all my might to retain my advanced placement level in math, private lessons and all, but eventually sufficed with the more average placement level. Luckily, however, I ended up scoring high on my Hebrew finals, mainly due to my mom's decision to send me to a Hebrew camp far from home. The camp's incredibly theatrical and captivating teacher, who went so far as to jump on tables, certainly sparked my interest.

***

My friends and I weren't aware that we were living in the country's periphery, mainly because we didn't have any other place to compare ourselves to. In the pre-social media era, having friends from a central city like Tel Aviv was practically impossible. We knew of nothing but the Golan Heights and its nearby towns. Living close to nature, it was natural to have a river running behind my house. It was our normal hangout spot after school, and when the sun would set, we'd go sit on the handrails by a quiet street. Using four stones, we made makeshift soccer goals outside of my friend's house, kicking the ball each afternoon in the hopes that none of the neighbors would complain about the noise. But the true highlight of our childhood was grabbing a burger at the McDonald's at the main junction about an hour away, a treat we'd be allowed once a month. For the most part, we played outside the house, and never once locked the door. Surely, growing up in Tel Aviv would have provided me with a radically different childhood.

Out of all the sports I played, basketball was my favorite. I read every related article in the sports column, collected cards, and knew the statistics about every NBA player. Never in my wildest dreams would I have imagined that one day, I'd be dancing on a table with one of them. We'll get to that later.

My basketball career kicked off when I was a kid in the local kids' league. My dad came to my games, cheering me on as he recorded all of the possible statistics, including assists (the apple doesn't fall far from the tree, as it were). I eventually made my way to my town's youth team, which played in the regional league. If I'm being honest, it wasn't that big of an achievement: there were no tryouts, and no one was ever told to pack their bags. All I had to do was not quit. The peak was in the 10th grade when we beat the mighty team from Tiberias. From that point on, it was all downhill. My sports career was short and sweet, and even included the title of runner-up in my school's tennis competition.

As we lived in the country's periphery, we were behind in practically everything. Cable TV was introduced into our homes nearly three years after the rest of the country had it. In that sense, it was tough living up north. If you wanted to take driving lessons, you had to leave the house hours before to hitchhike all the way down to the nearest city. If you were lucky enough to pass the driving test, your scope of potential hang-out spots expanded to a few new pubs – all, at the very least, an hour's drive from your house. But this all seemed natural to me back then. Today, now that I live on one of Tel Aviv's central streets, close to the sea and one step away from rows upon rows of bars and restaurants, I realize how disconnected we were.

On holiday vacations, I worked at whatever odd job I could get my hands on. I have a good friend, Adi Altschuler, who is always impressed by the diversity of my early resume. But for me, it was trivial – those were the only options I had.

I worked for a while in catering, where I got my first taste of foie gras (goose liver), by far the best thing I'd tasted until that point. I was paid minimum wage and did everything – dishwashing, seat arrangements, tidying up the tables, throwing out the trash – well, practically everything: I was never given the honor of waiting tables. Frankly, the person who'd let me serve customers would probably go bankrupt. I'm horribly clumsy.

Another odd job included working at a plastic manufacturing company, where I would stand on my feet for hours, meticulously examining the products, and making sure that no plastic box was left unchecked.

At the age of 16, I worked as a type of security guard at a popular beach on the Sea of Galilee. Sitting at the entrance to the shore, I had the power to decide who could go in or not. It seemed safe enough at the time, but today, I know I genuinely risked my life doing that job. There was no shortage of violence at the lake, including a stabbing incident I had to testify about at the police station.

Another, far less risky job, was working in a mango grove. Each day, at the crack of dawn, my friend Nadav and I, would turn up with our run-down cars (mine was a SEAT Malaga '86) and pick fresh mangos and litchi from the trees. As an expert in mangos, I'm happy to share this valuable piece of information with you: "Maya Mango," the round one with a light red blush, is the best kind.

The many jobs I dabbled in taught me that there is no such thing as dirty work.

***

Looking back at my childhood, I'm convinced that living in the countryside greatly benefited me as a person. It taught me how to appreciate the little things and instilled an unyielding thirst for progress. When you live in a remote area, you learn to enjoy whatever is at hand, and you're encouraged to work hard to reach your goals. After having to hitchhike from one car to the next to get to the nearest driving lesson, not only was multitasking as a college student a piece of cake, but, coming from a small place like Katzrin, life just seemed like a huge amusement park.

When I moved to Jerusalem for my bachelor's degree, I suffered from headaches due to the noise and complexities of the city. Only then did I realize how comforting green meadows and running rivers can be. I was raised by nature, in a place where values were set in stone, values I carry with me wherever I go.

Today, from the comfort of my home in the bustling city of Tel Aviv, I can still deeply appreciate the healing power nature has on the mind.

A Word to the Wise
by Nuseir Yassin (Nas Daily),
Renowned Vlogger

"We are much more than numbers"

I was told I was just a number, and since then, I've spent my whole life proving them otherwise.

As a 17-year-old boy from the village of Arraba, I wasn't sure what I wanted to do with my life. I'm convinced that you didn't either. I debated what to study, where to study, and why to study in the first place. Everyone insisted I needed to go to a university in Israel.

When I asked my teacher how one gets accepted into university in the first place, he replied, "It's simple, all you have to do is to score above 90 on your finals, and above 700 on your psychometric test. Taken together, these two numbers will determine what you can study. If they're high enough, you can become an engineer; if they're low, you can't even study engineering." Basically, we were told that these two numbers would dictate our careers and determine our financial situation in life.

How crazy is the world we live in? Why have we reduced humanity's potential to numbers? We are much more than numbers. We are living beings with unique personalities, a sense of humor, and aspirations – not a number on a standardized test.

That is the main reason I decided to flee this system and apply to Harvard University. There, they care about the person, not just the number. They asked me to send in an essay, along with a few recommendation letters, do an interview, and made me answer some crazy personal questions relating to my dreams and personality. Yes, they asked for numbers too.

So, at 17, I spent days upon days getting to know myself well, before submitting my candidacy to Harvard. "I am much more than numbers," I told Harvard, and offered them an innovative idea to transform the world's technology. To my surprise, they accepted me on a full scholarship! It was my ticket out of my small village in Israel. It was my chance to prove that people are much more than numbers, race, gender, or data points.

It was, undoubtedly, the best decision of my life.

As kids, we assume that the world is perfect: we are treated well by adults, Disney movies always have happy endings, and we are taught that good always prevails. For the most part, the world seems like a utopian place. But as we grow older, we realize the world is nothing close to a finished product. Certain systems need to be radically altered – from education to healthcare to raising the minimum wage.

You don't have to accept the system as it is. Always bear in mind that there's a way out. Once you release yourselves from its constraining grip, you can work on changing it for the better. Hopefully, you will be the change.

A Word to the Wise by
NETA RIVKIN,
Israeli rhythmic gymnast

"Don't waste energy on things you can't control"

The 2012 London Olympics was the second Olympics of my career. I was in the best shape of my life, but as one of the world's leading gymnasts, I felt an immeasurable amount of stress. I knew that this time, unlike the previous Olympics in Beijing where I was the youngest athlete in the Israeli delegation, more would be expected of me, including a finals appearance (in the top ten). Of course, my sights were set on a podium finish. On the flight to London, I remember telling myself: "Whatever you do, and however you do it, you're not coming home without a medal."

As the day of the competition grew closer, I felt a huge lump of anxiety build up inside me, a sign of impending doom. Unfortunately, my intuition was right. I kicked off the first day well, opening with an excellent hoop routine. But the following ball routine left me broken. While it started off smoothly, at one point the ball simply slipped out of my hands and rolled across the mat. And it kept rolling, all the way out of bounds. As I rushed to get it, all I could think about was running backstage and disappearing from the face of the Earth. Instead, I managed to pull myself together and returned to the mat to finish the performance.

In terms of the gravity of the error, this "small" mishap is every rhythmic gymnast's worst nightmare, and it happened to me during the most important competition of my career. When I walked off the mat, I saw nothing but black. Due to the extremely low score I was given, I found myself in 17th place, light years from the coveted top ten and a trip to the finals.

It took me several hours to process the abyss I'd fallen into, but after regaining my composure, I sat on my bed and made the decision to put whatever had happened behind me. It was time to look forward and see what I could do to lift myself in the standings with the time left. Two things were bound to happen the next day, two things I knew I had no control over. One – the score the judges would give me on my performance (I chose a pretty subjective branch in the Olympics, one that is hard to judge and comprises many variables). Two – what my competitors will bring to the mat.

I fully believe that each one of us has a limited amount of energy, and I decided I wouldn't waste even one iota of energy on the things I had no control over. For that reason, I spent the night focusing on the one thing that I had control over: my upcoming performance on the mat. It was a long night with little sleep and many reassuring mantras – *Tomorrow, I would reach the finals.* I woke up feeling positive, even though my fate was terribly uncertain due to my low starting point.

I walked onto the mat with an excellent clubs routine and finished with a clean, polished ribbon performance. Heading off stage, I was extremely nervous, even though

I knew I did the best I could. All I had to do now was wait for a score that was beyond my control.

Fortunately, this story had a happy ending: I placed ninth, securing my spot as a finalist. And in the finals, after the insane roller-coaster of the previous 24 hours, I competed with a sense of genuine tranquility and finished seventh. It was one of the best results in the delegation.

Back at home, after things cooled down – after the joy, euphoria, and heartwarming welcoming – I reflected on the nerve-racking series of events and learned a great deal about myself and life itself. The reason I managed to get myself out of that mental abyss was only because I succeeded in shifting my energy to the one area I had control over: my performance on the mat.

When we find ourselves in life-and-death situations, we discover our true strengths. In sports terms, I completely felt like I was somewhere between life and death. At that uncertain point, I discovered how strong I was, and how competent I was in coping with extreme situations. This event radically improved my self-esteem, and while I was happy with my place in the finals, I was happier knowing that I could fall down and climb back up on my own. If everything would've run smoothly in that Olympics, I don't think I would have been as proud.

CHAPTER 2

Between Lebanon and Malibu
How I learned I could sell anything

My own words failed me, ruining my chances of becoming a Mossad agent. With the naive honesty of an 18-year-old boy, I sat in a bland apartment in a suburb of Tel Aviv and told the interviewer evaluating me for a job in the intelligence agency all about my ADHD and dysgraphia. I candidly shared the unclear writing, mixed-up letters, and plenty of spelling errors that came with it. I was furious with myself after the interview. In truth, reflecting on it today, I wouldn't have accepted that boy either.

I think I landed that interview due to my foreign citizenship (thank you Mom, for my Canadian passport!). To my credit, I can say that my interviewing skills have improved over the years, and I now know what to say and what not to say, but I surely wasn't born with these abilities.

To this day, I believe I could've been a great chameleon.

I know how to read different situations and adapt myself accordingly, as well as talk people into following me, in the most subtle manner possible. Either way, it's clear that things turned out for the best. I'm glad I didn't become a Mossad agent.

For boys coming from the north of Israel, the selection process for the Israeli Defense Forces was held at the recruitment office in Tiberias, on the shores of the Sea of Galilee, and always ended at one of the incredible falafel stands in the center of town. With a mere five shekels, you could get half a portion – a mouth-watering dish served with French fries and a variety of salads (getting the full portion for eight shekels wasn't worth it because everyone knew the add-ons and side dishes were the best part). This explained the long, outstretched lines. At our regional high school, whose many students came from *kibbutzim*[1] and *moshavim* (Israeli cooperative agricultural communities), the path was clearly steered toward combat service. Any other position was out of the question. Like many of my friends, I attended the assessment day for several of the army's more prestigious units but ended up failing the theoretical exam to become a naval officer and the tryouts to become a paratrooper. Ultimately, in March of 2001, I reported on my draft day, unsure of where I was headed.

On the very same day, recruitment for the Border Police was being held, causing my mom and me a slight panic. Thankfully, we found out this was also the day

---

1. The plural of "kibbutz" in Hebrew (the suffix "im" denotes the plural form).

they were recruiting for combat intelligence. Along with Sagi, the only other "northern" boy there with me, I was sent to boot camp with a group of combat engineer soldiers in a remote training base about 40 minutes away from Eilat (Israel's southernmost city, and as far as can be from Katzrin). Out of the 48-hour furlough I'd receive, 16 of them were spent on the road, mostly on the famous Route 843 that travels from Tel Aviv to the north and passes through every possible shithole on the way. This legendary route even starred in an Israeli comedy skit as the "never-ending bus line." If it wasn't for my parents, who picked me up from the junction near our house, my furlough would have been practically nonexistent.

I was surrounded by incredible guys, sharp and interesting, but as an easily overwhelmed newcomer, it took me a while to get adjusted to the army. I don't often excel in things that come easy to others, like handiwork, which in the army is required for equipment and gear upkeep. I don't like it, nor do I spend the time to get better at it. To this day, I can't hammer a nail straight or change a busted lightbulb. However, I'm a complete enthusiast when it comes to things I am good at, and I enjoy letting others do what they know best as well. A form of outsourcing, I would say. In general, life has taught me that I'd rather pay professionals to do jobs I'm not good at, instead of wasting time learning them myself. It's a valuable life lesson: focus on developing new skills, while simultaneously investing your time and energy in improving existing ones. This lesson, however, wasn't applicable in the army. Even if fixing gear wasn't my forte, I wasn't left with much choice but to do it.

On one of my weekends off, drained and exhausted – only now do I understand how tired we were those Friday nights, driving long distances to parties in the area – I called my friend Dror to see what he was doing. Unknowingly, I ended up calling the name before his on my contact list. Out of all the names on the list, I called David, one of my army commanders, who sounded utterly confused when I snapped, "Come on, you asshole, don't you recognize me?" By the time I realized my mistake, it was too late. That horribly pointless sentence shortened my next furlough; news handed to me two days later by David himself on a bright Sunday morning at the Bedouin market in Beersheba as we waited for the busses taking us to boot camp. After calling us to stand in formation, David (failing to hide the smug grin under his ginger beard) said, "Rivlin, don't you recognize me?"

Boot camp was the place I began learning more about the world, or better put, Israel. I met guys from all over the country, and for the first time in my life, went out to places I'd only heard about in hushed tones, like the TLV club at the port in Tel Aviv.

We finished boot camp at that God-forsaken base and then moved on to advanced training somewhere else, specifically focusing on intelligence-related aspects. This was one of the most grueling yet empowering periods of my service. We went on long forced marches that tested the boundaries of our bodies and minds. That feeling of immeasurable strength, of pushing forward under extreme conditions, kicked my self-esteem up another notch and has stayed with me to this day.

I was assigned to a team that served up north near the

border with Lebanon (and close to my house). We drove the "Raccoon," a modified Hummer with special surveillance equipment. Unlike the other teams that were placed in stationary outposts, our team moved around from target to target. I couldn't have dreamt of a better placement than that, a kind of preparation for the life that awaited me – I very much enjoy being on the move as opposed to being static. Another great thing that came out of the army was the operational driving course to which I was sent – three weeks of off-road driving from sunrise to sunset with troops from various commando units, and a handy truck license to top it off. Just to revisit that guy who entered the army as a dazed and confused kid, changing a flat tire in the mud at two a.m., in the pouring rain – well, that really wasn't him. But I learned the fundamentals and got the job done. Somehow, my partner from the Paratrooper Brigade's most elite unit couldn't cut it and was dropped. To this day, I have no idea how I made it and he didn't. The course taught me that I could do anything, even things I didn't want to.

I returned to my team as an operational Raccoon driver until I was sent off again, this time to attend a commander's course. I didn't feel I was the best soldier in the IDF, but I certainly gave it an interesting shot. Ultimately, I returned to where it all began, the base where I did my basic training, but this time as a sergeant for a fresh team of recruits. I don't enjoy writing up equipment lists and making sure nothing gets lost; it doesn't come naturally to me. But to my surprise, I did a pretty good job at it. I was deployed up north with the team I helped train and, being mobile, we were able to move between the various lookout posts full of female soldiers (a rare and non-trivial treat for combat soldiers). When it came to girls, though, my confidence was still low. I remember sitting with a female soldier one night, a spotter at one of the surveillance posts, only later realizing that she wanted me to kiss her. When it was time for the reserves, I was attached to my old Combat Intelligence Unit (*Yahmam*) and served on the elite team that crossed into Lebanon at the outset of the Second Lebanon War, 24 years after I was born into the first one.

By the time I finished the army, I was a completely different person. Not only had I broadened my understanding of Israel, but also of myself. The guy who left the army at the age of 21 had far more confidence than the 18-year-old boy who was drafted three years earlier. I was even dating my first girlfriend, Chen. Unfortunately, it was also my first time dealing with grief and loss. I had never been to a funeral before, and suddenly, I found myself at cemeteries.

Elkana Gobi, a friend from my unit with golden hair and blue eyes, had fallen in battle. He was posthumously awarded for his inspiring initiative, determination and courage, when, while on vacation, driving down the highway with his two brothers, he spotted a terrorist shooting civilian cars passing by. Elkana stopped his car on the side of the road and opened fire at a terrorist who fled the scene. A standby military force in the area spotted Elkana, laying on the ground in civilian clothes and shooting, and mistook him for the terrorist. Tragically, they ran him over.

In the middle of advanced training, my dad called to tell me that Ron Lavi, a childhood friend of mine and one of the smartest people I knew, was killed when his Merkava tank hit an explosive device on the outskirts of Gaza in the pursuit of a terrorist. If there was one guy who could rightfully argue with me about statistics, it was Ron, an avid fan of Manchester United and the person with whom I shared my love of basketball. We played together and watched countless games over the years. Around the same time, a girl who went to school with me named Sari Goldstein was murdered in August 2002 when a terrorist blew himself up on the bus she boarded.

All of these events, at such a young age, granted me a radically new perspective on life.

***

The army taught me that one could get the most out of anything, even from experiences that are forced upon us. Apparently, we can enjoy pushing our bodies to the limit on long, tiring marches covering dozens of miles, as well as driving on missions across muddy fields and changing flat tires in the dead of night. Pursuing combat service has its benefits. While coveted intelligence corps units (like 8200) set one on a pretty clear-cut path, giving rise to a sense of certainty (similar to the feeling when studying law or medicine), the value of combat service relies heavily on one's own initiative. It is more challenging because it requires that you pave your own way, but that's also what makes it fascinating. I feel like if they did a comparative study on graduates of intelligence units and graduates of combat units, they would find that the progression of combat soldiers in different stages of life is much more diverse. Of course, each path has its own unique qualities, the question is which one is right for you, and what you can get out of it. What's more, the choice is often not in your hands anyway. There's no reason not to take advantage of the opportunity at hand, even if we didn't choose it.

I viewed military service as a kind of game, for better or worse. It's a game that teaches you a host of new skills, and from which you leave far more mature and better equipped.

There's a saying I like that I heard from one of my professors at Harvard, Ronald Heifetz. He would say, "Take a step to the balcony," which means, whatever you come across, take a bird's eye view of it; take your time, make good use of it, embrace the opportunities that come your way, and learn how to articulate and unpack those things in the best way possible. The commander's course I did and the truck license I earned were gifts. You never know when they might come in handy.

A good example of this is the story of a good friend of mine, Yael Wissner-Levy, who was a bored soldier guarding and scanning the country's northern border when she happened to meet a senator from Arizona named John McCain, who she was unfamiliar with. Accompanied by an IDF spokesperson and a combat officer with broken English, it was 19-year-old Yael who enthusiastically walked the guests through the views appearing on the camera screen. This chance meeting, between the young soldier and the future candidate of the Republican Party for the presidency of the United States, and the one who would lose the race to Barack Obama, introduced Yael to the world of diplomacy. Following her meeting with the senator, and upon her release from the army, Yael decided to work for the American Congress, a decision that paved her way later on. She wrote speeches for senior figures in the political world, including former Israeli president Shimon Peres. And today, after shifting to the world of business, she is the VP of Communications at Lemonade, one of the most successful Israeli start-ups, and has entered the esteemed list of newspapers defining the country's 40 most influential people under the age of 40. Her career path took off in the army due to one random encounter with Senator McCain.

***

Toward the end of my military service, I applied for counselor positions for the Jewish Agency's summer camps around the U.S. I planned on seeing the world and liked the idea of having someone fund my travels while spreading Zionist values in return. My fluency in English, as well as my brief career as a basketball player, made me stand out from the crowd. Not only was I accepted, but I was placed in one of the most coveted camps: JCA Shalom in Malibu, California. My closest neighbor was none other than Pamela Anderson, and the other counselors and I spent a good amount of time outside the camp trying to catch a glimpse of her, albeit unsuccessfully.

It was the year 2004, and I had some time between my

discharge from the army in March and the start of the camp in the summer, so I decided to make good use of it and study for the daunting psychometric test (the Israeli equivalent of the SATs). After attending a preparatory course each Friday for several weeks, I ended up with a less-than-dazzling score of 542 (out of 800). I was disappointed. While I didn't expect to get a perfect score, I did believe I'd get at least a little lucky. Ashamed of my score, it took me years before I revealed it to anybody. It sparked a flurry of self-doubt: Am I good enough? What if they find out I'm just bluffing? What does this mean about me? Will I make it in life? Back then, I didn't know what I wanted to study yet. In fact, I still haven't figured that out. It really doesn't matter that much.

In June 2004, I flew to the summer camp in Malibu, a place that looked picture perfect: wooden cabins in a remote forest, activities galore, and parties all around. Indeed, the movie "Band Camp" in the "American Pie" franchise was filmed there. On Friday evening, everyone wore white and marched after Robo the guitarist who played Jewish Sabbath songs. On Saturday, as the weekend ended, we would eat pizza with ice cream and peanut butter on the side. On "Israel Day," as the young crowd of American children stared at us mesmerized, we, the staff, wore army uniforms and discussed our experiences as soldiers. Days off would include trips to Disneyland or meetups at the houses of the other American counselors, which looked more like palaces than places where real people lived. Overall, it was an eye-opening American experience that I dove into whole-heartedly and enjoyed, knowing fully well that the experience wouldn't change itself for me, rather, I'd need to adjust myself to it and accept whatever comes. And if I happened to be at the summer camp in Malibu, then that meant dancing at parties and making out in the woods with the other counselors.

The Malibu camp was the start of a global perspective I was developing. I made use of my advantages to become a Jewish Agency emissary, and from that point onwards, things progressed, step after step. Along with the Israeli counselors, I wrapped up the summer camp with a road trip from Los Angeles to San Francisco on Highway 1, one of the most breathtaking roads in the world, in my view.

Driven to make as much money as I could for traveling, I used my Canadian passport to fly and visit my late aunt Helen, my mother's sister, who lived in the Forest Hill neighborhood in midtown Toronto. My cousin, Jill, hooked me up with a comfortable job in customer service at a toy company called Spin Master, which back then was a fairly small company and is now worth billions. The company's line of Air Hogs – remote-controlled cars and helicopters – took over North America, and my job was to answer emails sent by angry customers complaining about the product. The company was founded by Jews, one of them, Ronen Harrary, a former Israeli whose mom spoiled us in the office with cream cheese and salmon bagels. I'm not going to lie, I had shifts where I'd scarf down three of those bagels or more. Healthy eating was beyond me at the time.

In my search for additional income, I ran into Lazer, a religious Canadian Jew who became fast friends with my incredibly outgoing and affable aunt Helen, after they happened to meet at the mall. Lazer was the owner of several kiosks selling Dead Sea products at malls. This job was tailor-made for Israelis with the "chutzpah" or, in other words, the audacity, to stop someone in the mall and try and sell them a product they never even considered buying. I want to talk about the word "chutzpah" for a moment. Many people see it as something negative, but I actually think it has some positive aspects to it. Everyone needs to have a certain amount of "chutzpah," or at least the proper dosage, of course.

As a Canadian citizen, I had an advantage as a salesperson. I got a 30% sales commission, instead of the 25% non-Canadians received. Curious to see if I'd be good at it, I tried it and was thrown head-deep into the water. Come on, start selling. With no previous experience in sales, I gradually became one of the best salesmen of Dead Sea products in North America, a title that is definitely worth noting.

My starting point was good: I was placed in Yorkdale Mall, one of the busiest ones in the province. My shifts were either on weekends or at the end of a long day working in Spin Master's customer service department. Dreading the idea of ending a shift without a sale, I learned how to do it well, and polished my skills in the field. Wearing a white suit that gave an air of professionalism, I exhausted my natural reserves of patience and geniality as I regaled Miss Canadian shopper with the amazing attributes of our nail files and wondrous healing powers of the Dead Sea. If she liked the nail file, I always managed to sell her another something on top. Full of motivation and determination to discover the inner workings of customers, to figure out what made each one tick, I learned to spot potential clients in a matter of seconds – from the way they walked, their facial expression, their Louis Vuitton bag, their ethnicity, whether they wore a kippah (or yarmulke) on their head. I could even spot Jewish women who hadn't visited the Holy Land in a while. Whenever I managed a sale, my self-confidence skyrocketed; yet another step up the ladder of success. The peak of the season was Christmas, a time of grueling yet satisfying 20-hour shifts.

The thought of working in sales scares many of us. We feel uncomfortable selling, and we might even see it as some sort of fraud. We forget that it's all a matter of demand and supply: if people are willing to pay an amount that is 15 times higher than the actual cost, then they probably really want that product. In that case, the decision is theirs, not yours. All of this is based on the condition that you're okay with what you're selling – do not sell a product you don't believe in.

At the end of the day, life is one big sales show. We spend our whole lives – consciously or unconsciously – marketing ourselves. Most of our jobs focus on selling something. If not a product, then ourselves, who we are, our story. If you're a good salesperson – and I don't mean it in the somewhat negative or cheap way it might be perceived – it can give you a serious advantage in many fields. Each person, no matter what they do, needs to work on their sales skills. The sales element is an ongoing theme in life, and whoever does it well can capitalize on any situation. Find your edge in sales and use it well. For example, I know I'm bad at selling myself through writing. Knowing that, I worked on this book with a ghostwriter and an incredible editor who helped translate my thoughts into words.

With enough money saved up, I left Canada behind, as well as my then-girlfriend, Dafna (my grandma's neighbor in Montreal and whose parents are Israeli), and headed on a trip around Central America. Looking back, I should have broken up with Dafna before I left, as I would have felt a lot freer traveling. My trip began in Guatemala, where I spent a month exploring the green landscape. Despite my daily interaction with locals, I failed to learn Spanish in Antigua, a defeat that brought to the surface thoughts about my average high school grades and low psychometric test. Putting that aside, I enjoyed trekking, being on the roads in crowded buses full of chickens and meeting fellow Israeli travelers along the way.

My next station was Mexico, a place I still have regrets about for not seeing the potential it had back then. In 2004, Tulum was a beautiful city on the Caribbean side, with white pristine shores, turquoise waters, palm trees, and ancient ruins from the Mayan civilization peppered along the hills. It was a quiet place with a few hostels, and it was obvious that it would soon explode and become a paradise for real estate investors. Indeed, today it's packed with hotels. I have no doubt that the return has now increased 100-fold. Ever since, I've believed that anyone with a good eye will put his money in places where young Israelis, fresh from the army, go traveling, because they are always searching for the best deals, and are among the first ones to find out about the places that will soon become coveted tourist spots.

I finished the trip in Cuba, a destination that wasn't very common at the time. It felt like time-traveling backward to a country that had been frozen in time since the 1950s. A country with two currency types – one for tourists and one for locals. A country where, despite its scarcity of resources, people always seemed happy, playing music and dancing in the streets – valid proof that money doesn't buy happiness.

The combination of people and ever-changing views, and the ability to be spontaneous and live in the moment for days on end, can be a wild ride. Still, I walked the typical route most Israeli tourists take but managed to find my own way within it.

Today, I'd recommend walking the path unknown, and if possible, travel alone – at least in the beginning. It adds a different quality to the experience, forcing you to open up to the world. It wasn't until the next trip I took that I learned not to waste time bargaining – a very Israeli thing to do – over nickels and dimes that would yield me a minuscule profit (even though bargaining is a very important skill that adds to one's sense of accomplishment). Overall, you can enjoy a lot more if you learn to let go. In this case, as with many others, I should have "stepped out onto the balcony" and relaxed.

***

After three months of traveling, I got back with Dafna, who was waiting for me in Montreal, and she joined me in Israel as part of a student exchange program from Tel Aviv University. I rented a flat in Tel Aviv with a roommate, and Dafna lived nearby in the student dorms. To my already eclectic work resume, I added being a counselor at a daycare, where I learned what true patience was.

The big city was a place I never pictured myself living in, and I felt like a complete outsider. The plan was to study at a college close to home up north, an idea crafted either because the program I got accepted to (a blend of political science, finance, and sociology) interested me, or because I believed that a small, local college suited me more than a big university. I don't remember why, but I still decided to enroll at the Hebrew University in Jerusalem, despite my low psychometric score. As Israeli universities put all their emphasis on grades, one of the only tracks I could apply for with that score was sociology and political science (despite longing for the desirable philosophy, politics, and economics track).

Still, on a last-minute whim, I chose the Hebrew University. Longing to experience something completely different from where I grew up, it was clear to me that the university would provide experiences I wouldn't find in a local college. The fact that several people I traveled with also studied there added to my decision to go for it. It was a wise choice at a crucial crossroads in my life: if I would've chosen the college up north – no disrespect intended – I probably wouldn't have made it this far. I would have stayed up north, not only geographically, but also spiritually, stunting my growth by keeping me in my comfort zone. I chose to get out there and explore.

My Word to the Wise

- Take advantage of every opportunity, even ones that were forced upon you – like mandatory courses in the university, family responsibilities, or military service, and make the most out of it.
- Sought-after routes, like joining a coveted military unit or attending the most prestigious college, might open doors to a promising career, but don't belittle opportunities that are less esteemed – they may take you elsewhere, and who knows, potentially some place better.
- Traveling the world, whether alone or with friends, is highly recommended. But don't rush to run along the well-known path, rather, find the path that is right for you, even if it's less crowded.
- Sales are an inseparable part of life. No matter what you do, you will always need to sell something. Sharpen your marketing skills, find your strengths and use them wisely to get ahead.
- Finally, no matter where you are, immerse yourself in the present moment and experience it to the fullest.

A Word to the Wise by STAV SHAFFIR,
FORMER ISRAELI MP AND FOUNDER OF THE "SHIRA CENTER" — AN ACADEMIC INSTITUTE FOR PEOPLE WITH SPECIAL NEEDS

"Don't wait for experience to make things happen"

When I joined the Knesset's Finance Committee, I was the youngest, most inexperienced member of parliament. Stepping in as a representative of the prevailing social movement, I was afraid to make mistakes, feeling like every error of mine would serve as proof for those who accused the young protesters of naïveté and ignorance.

The first few months were spent with my head down, studying, and pouring over stacks of documents late into the night so I could come prepared for the following day's meetings. One day, after being called in for a special deliberation, I came across a pile of papers with state budget charts I hadn't seen before.

"What is this?" I asked, but all I got was an aloof shrug of the shoulders from my colleagues. I thought I might have missed a prefatory email on the topic.

"Of course not," the committee chairman replied, "we don't discuss these things over emails."

I continued probing, "Mr. Chairman, what exactly are we voting on?"

The chairman waved his hand in disregard and announced, "Just some technical issues. A quick vote and we can all go home."

As one of the impatient committee members urged us to speed things along, I couldn't help dwelling over the word "technical," which echoed in my mind like an alarm. I skimmed through the budget tables rapidly, reading through substantial cutbacks in funds pertaining to both the ministry of education and public transportation. None of the committee members knew what they were voting for, yet, in a matter of minutes, billions of dollars were about to be transferred straight from the public's pocket to places beyond anyone's knowledge.

As it turns out, this had been going on for years. I asked the chairman to stop the vote so we could go over things carefully. Fortunately, several other members backed me up, and the chairman had no other choice but to comply. I ran back to my office and, with the help of my team, I scanned and uploaded the budget charts to Facebook so the public could see what was happening with their money. Within 24 hours, 120 volunteers had joined me in reviewing the files. By the time we convened again, I had numerous questions for the committee. We dug and prodded the government's representatives down to the smallest details. And wow, the things we found...

"You're a little girl who doesn't understand anything," I was told on several occasions, to scare me from asking more questions. But I ignored them and carried on. When someone is intimidated by questions, there's a good chance they're hiding something. "You're risking your political reputation," older members of the committee would often whisper in my ear, but that motivated me even more. Within a few months, I exposed the state's mind-boggling corruption amounting to billions of dollars.

The system had been working like this for years, serving the interests of a few greedy politicians who viewed the Knesset and public service as an opportunity to divert funds in order to accumulate power. Nearly everyone went along with it. Thus, year after year, our money would be taken and used for purposes that don't serve the public, while social services were slashed unimpeded. By exposing the budget, we made it – for the first time in history – transparent. This transparency, bringing it to the light, allowed us to put an end to this misappropriation of public funds. Our actions put the state's politicians on notice and made them understand they were under the watchful eye of the public and couldn't keep doing as they wished with the budget. We put a stop to massive levels of corruption.

Exposing some of the most powerful people in the country came with threats and attacks. But the more we were harassed, the more confident I felt that we were on the right track. After a year of investigation, we submitted a petition to the Supreme Court proving the illegality of this method. And so, as the youngest and most inexperienced member of the Knesset, I found myself negotiating with the government on ways to change the system. The finance committee was forced to establish new procedures to ensure public transparency. Following the events, the Organization for Economic Cooperation and Development (OECD) invited me to manage a transparency committee comprising dozens of parliamentarians from around the world who gathered to determine new standards for public transparency. We knew deep down that we were advancing the revolution on the public's behalf – making politics more transparent and trustworthy.

Today, while we still have a lot more work to do, one thing is clear: if I would have kept on doing what others told me to, I wouldn't have uncovered even one layer of the system impacting nearly every aspect of our lives. If we wait for work experience to dictate whether we take bold steps to change things; if we wait until we're more "qualified," we might forget what we wanted to do in the first place. At times, the places in which we stick out like a sore thumb are exactly where we are needed most. At the end of the day, what people think of us is not as important as what we came to do, and no matter who tries to steer us off the path, we will keep marching boldly toward our goals.

CHAPTER 3

Jerusalem, the Hebrew University
Good thing I didn't study medicine

I like to think of universities as amusement parks full of opportunities. Everything is open for you to explore; all you have to do is dare. Will you choose to swing idly on the safest swing, or will you ride the wildest rollercoaster, hop on the dark tunnel ride with a mystery waiting for you at the other end, or take the spinning carousel propelling you to personal heights previously unknown? All you have to do is get familiar with the rides and muster the courage to buckle in. For me, the Hebrew University wasn't just a fun amusement park, it was a fantastic springboard from which I jumped out into the "real world."

In many cases – too many – students don't take enough advantage of their time at university. They overlook the potential of that novel period in life. Instead, they stick to what they know, their comfort zone. Moving out of the house, for example, far from home, not choosing the closest college, and expanding your social circle by living among other students in a shared dorm or apartment, is one of the best things you can do. For those of you who think it's wiser to stay at your parent's house and save money – I'm not buying it.

No one will convince me that it's better to work a convenient student job that pays relatively well over a worse-paying job that adds experience and enhances their resume. Don't misunderstand me, I have all the respect in the world for student jobs, but let's be honest, they rarely have long-term professional benefits.

No one will convince me that attending Political Science 101 with three-hundred students in a large, disengaging hall is a good use of one's time, even if the view of the Dead Sea and Judean Desert is spectacular. Students are better off going to small classes where actual interaction happens. Intro courses are important, but they can definitely be self-taught.

The Israeli student is notably different than the average 18-year-old American going to college. Unlike the latter, Israelis are normally 22-23 when they first start, and chances are they have spent the last few months traveling the world after the army. Unlike the American student, Israelis will most likely work part-time and juggle both endeavors, as it would be a waste to do nothing but study. The university serves as somewhat of a break from life, a transitional period from before "real life" begins and you take your first steps in the job market. As a student, you're still free of society's judgments and criticisms. It is a uniquely ephemeral juncture in life where one can, and should, dive in and try what they can – share a dorm room with a stranger, shower in communal bathrooms, write a bill proposal for the construction of the Third Jewish Temple, shoot a movie with a Palestinian student, or embark on a series of lectures around the U.S. (I'll get into all of that later). These experiences can have an immense impact on your life if only you'd pick your head up out of the books for a minute and make do with a slightly lower grade point average. There are far more beneficial things on which to focus.

If life is a journey, then your twenties is your springboard to the bigger world. It is when you discover your uniqueness, a time of growth and development. But this doesn't come effortlessly; it is important to maximize the platform this sanctuary provides. Bear in mind that big universities can, at times, offer you more – in terms of opportunities, professors, and social circles – as opposed to smaller schools which may seem more inviting for other reasons. It's important to choose a university that pushes you forward. There's a phrase in Hebrew that I believe suits this dilemma: would you rather be *a head to the foxes, or a tail to the lions*? Which is to say, would you rather be the leader of a weak group, or play a minor role in a strong, powerful one? If you start out as the tail of a lion, you can work your way up until you become a lion yourself, but if you start out as head of the foxes, how much more can you grow?

The truth of the matter is, what you choose to study isn't especially important, unless you're aiming at some defined profession like medicine, social work, or engineering. To put it into numbers: 20% of your degree involves studying, 30% involves the people you meet (some of my best friends today went to undergrad school with me), and 50% involves all the extra-curricular activities. I'm a huge advocate of higher education, as long as one studies what actually interests them and sparks their curiosity.

We tend to put too much weight on our choice of major and carry that heavy burden with us on our backs. The decision is far less dramatic than we think. You chose the wrong track? You're not enjoying yourself? It's not the end of the world and totally fixable. Take the lessons with you and pick a different major. Figure out what you really like, what excites you, what you really want to study, and when you find the right answer, pick a school that will grant you not only a degree but a lot more.

***

Throughout all my years in academia, including at Harvard, I never had to spend a dime on tuition. I funded all my studies with the help of scholarships. I paid for my undergrad degree with a special scholarship given to combat soldiers from the periphery. In return, I volunteered at a non-profit organization working with children at risk and was paired with 12-year-old Andrei – the only child of a single mom who fled the former Soviet Union and immigrated to Israel. Together, we spent hours playing soccer, working on his homework, and talking about life.

This scholarship didn't come out of the blue. I searched and searched until I found the right one for me. There are plenty of scholarships out there, you just have to find them and capitalize on your advantages (place of residence, socioeconomic status, military service, etc.). Hunting for a scholarship is not an easy task, and it requires quite a lot of time and effort to understand what is out there and which one might suit you, but it's worth it. It's better to look for new scholarships, ones that don't have as many applicants. And even though you might get rejected along the way, keep going – all you need is one positive answer to fund your tuition and make your life easier.

My first steps in Jerusalem were taken at the Reznik dormitories at the Mount Scopus campus, just a stone's throw from the classrooms, where I shared a tiny room with Sagi, a psychology major. Our bathroom was located on the men's communal floor, where we piled in with several other students. The lucky ones were those at the Idelson dorms who had their very own bathrooms. Living in a dorm was an unforgettable and invaluable experience, even though, looking back today, I have no idea how I did it. I suppose such conditions are best suited to people in their twenties, when memories of the army are still fresh and just about anything seems like an upgrade.

At any rate, living in a dorm and being surrounded by a group of diverse and interesting people – great partners for cheese and wine nights – was an experience like no other and one that I seriously recommend, at least for the first year. In the U.S., incidentally, freshmen are obligated to live in dorms, and I can understand why.

On my first trip to the university's library, I met Tomer Avital, who is now an activist and independent journalist, and one of my best friends. Together with Lora, Yaniv Blum, and Idan – all students of political science who lived in my dorm – we became a group of friends who nourished and challenged each other.

As the descendant of a proud Jerusalem family (former President Reuven "Ruby" Rivlin is my father's cousin) who were among the first to venture beyond the Old City's walls, and whose last name appears on a street and square, I was excited to be in such a historical city. I wanted to experience as much of it as possible. The late Etti Rivlin, Ruby's sister and my father's cousin, a former Etzel[2] fighter and a woman who didn't believe in cars, took me on fascinating walking tours around the city.

I hung out quite a lot on Rivlin Street, spending evenings with friends in a neighborhood packed with American tourists. At the time, Tel Aviv felt distant, as if it was part of a completely different world. With just a one-hour car ride separating the two, Tel Aviv and Jerusalem could not be more different. But as much as I fell in love with Jerusalem, it's hard to picture myself going back. Where you live really depends on your current situation in life, and as such, it has the potential to open you up to so many different worlds. I never would have imagined that by the time I'd reach forty, I'd have lived in so many different places, in Israel, and around the globe.

My first year was spent studying, understanding how the university works and making friends. This is the

---

2. The Etzel, or Irgun, was a Zionist paramilitary organization that operated in Mandatory Palestine between 1931 and 1948.

right way to go into any new situation: immerse yourself, observe, look inward to find what feels right, and from that point of stability, take action. Tomer Avital, who was always one step ahead of me, joined the leadership program of OneVoice, a movement representing the moderate majority in Israel and the Palestinian Authority, which strives for a shared future grounded on values of security, justice, and respect. As a person with a clear political agenda, who wholeheartedly believes in this vision, this program fascinated me and I was happy to be accepted.

I was equally fascinated by the fact that Jason Alexander, "Seinfeld's" very own George Costanza, was a member of the program's advising committee. I thought of him later on in life when I tried to figure out what attracts people to organizations and these kinds of causes. The program's manager at the time was Adi Balderman, a good friend of mine today and my partner on the board of OneDay, an NGO whose goal is to create new and significant volunteering opportunities for young people.

When I first joined the program, OneVoice was just starting out. Being as it was new, there was a lot more room to make an impact if done right, and it was crucial to be there in those pivotal moments. We held intimate dinner meetings with the founder, Daniel Lubetzky – an inspiring entrepreneur, author and activist, and the billionaire founder of snack company Kind LLC – where he let us in on his life story, from his early beginnings in Mexico to the motivation behind doing business and promoting peace simultaneously. Together with Astar Yadid, I founded OneVoice's first student chapter, which later expanded to other campuses across the country. Among other endeavors, we organized meetings between One Voice's Palestinian activists and Hebrew University students.

Along the way, I was chosen for a pilot program called "Who Am I," helmed by Steven Spielberg, an avid supporter of the organization. As part of the program, ten Israelis and ten Palestinians were given video cameras and instructed to record their daily lives, in the hopes that their recordings would bridge two conflicting communities. The pilot kicked off in 2006, the year Facebook began spreading across the world (though it hadn't reached Israel yet). In the absence of social networks, it was nearly impossible to get a glimpse of the other person's life, all the more so if they were considered your enemy. So we spent two weeks recording, and with the help of a professional editor, squeezed it all into a five-minute video. This short clip was then passed on from the Israeli participants to their Palestinian partners, who replied with their own short video, thus creating a ping-pong of clips between participants.

My partner for the program was Tarek from Ramallah, whose family was connected to Yasser Arafat. Tarek told me stories of his life in Ramallah, endearing moments with his friends and girlfriend. In return, I told him about life in Jerusalem, my friends, and the girl I was dating at the time, Shahar. Through this program, we were able to prove, quite easily, that the distance between Jerusalem and Ramallah wasn't that great (literally and figuratively), and that despite coming from opposing nations, the lifestyle, aspirations, and dreams of two young people around the same age are quite similar. As we neared the final recording, Tarek visited my apartment in Jerusalem (by my second year of school I had left the dorms in favor of rooming with friends Omrit and Hadar from my trip to Central America), and at the end of our shared video session, I walked him to his appointment at a nearby tattoo shop.

During my time with OneVoice, I took part in another film where I'm seen overlooking Syria from Mount Bental (right before the civil war erupted there) and discussing my dreams of eating hummus one day in Damascus.

I'm a huge proponent of trying to understand the other side, of practicing empathy that allows for progress, even in complex situations. While it's easy to put up roadblocks between us and "the other," we must remember that the other side has an abundance of life as rich and important as ours, and there's no way to access it without genuine empathy. Honest social relations are those that lead to real change. In fact, Forbes magazine chose empathy as the single most important quality a leader can have, and I fully agree with that choice, because being a leader entails seeing things from multiple perspectives.

At around the same time, I joined an internship program offered by the university that assigned students to various institutions in Jerusalem based on their fields of study and interest. It was one of those win-win types of programs in which I so deeply believe: I didn't get paid for the internship, but instead, was rewarded with professional experience and skills I wouldn't have otherwise received doing a basic student job. During my run with OneVoice, I met Alon Nouriel, an Israeli political advisor from the Sephardic ultra-Orthodox "Shas" party, who introduced me to fellow politician Ya'akov Margi, who would later head the Ministry of Religious Services. This kind of mingling is prevalent in nonprofits and other organizations and is an excellent way to create effective bonds that will help you in the future.

Back in the university's amusement park of opportunities, I was given the chance to take part in something I had never pictured myself doing – serving as the legislative assistant to the parliamentary advisor of an ultra-Orthodox politician. This special stature gave me an advantage: the second parliamentary advisor also served as a driver, so my options to stand out were greater. Among other endeavors, I wrote Ya'akov Margi a bill for... the construction of the Third Jewish Temple. While this topic didn't really resonate with me, working on it with a religious political party expanded my views and shed light on a sector I didn't know much about. Moreover, the experience and knowledge I gained as a legislative assistant to the chairman of a large political party upgraded my resume considerably. Margi helped me later in life, after he'd already been appointed minister, by writing me letters of recommendation for the prestigious "Sauvé Scholars" scholarship program in Canada and Harvard (which we'll discuss further in the next chapter). I'm also sure that recommendation letters from someone whose beliefs are so different from my own went a long way in convincing these institutions that I was ready and mature enough to leave my comfort zone.

Thanks to this internship – which, I remind you, I volunteered for – I was chosen, along with Shadha

Muslim from Hebron, to represent OneVoice in a series of talks in Washington. Each one of us was asked to share their life story and discuss their agenda. I talked about my upbringing in the Golan Heights, where I dreamed of making peace with Syria one day, as well as my time in the army as a combat soldier who was shaken by loss but still fully believed in a better future.

Landing in Washington, we were given a kind and warm welcome by Mimi and Laurel, representatives of the organization in the U.S., and along with Shadha, I lectured before large crowds of university students, members of Congress, and an audience of 25,000 people at a rally. The feeling of shock that accompanied my first lecture gradually faded over time, and it was replaced by a pleasant sensation, satisfied with being able to convey my message in a captivating way. We're not born with public speaking skills, but we have the chance to improve over time and appear more natural with the help of guidance and training. Shadha and I were interviewed for the Washington Times, and Daniel Lubetzky wrote about us in the Huffington Post. These two articles, published in two major media outlets, substantially helped me to get ahead later on in life.

The tour I did in Washington was an eye-opening experience for me, a then-25-year-old student: I slept in fancy hotels, met with representatives of Congress, and spoke in front of a huge audience about crucial things I believed in with all my heart. By virtue of those moments, I began building my reputation, step by step. If I had Googled my name back then, I would have surely been proud of what came up, and that was only the start of it.

***

During my second year in school, I applied to coordinate a joint program of the Hebrew University's Rothberg School for International Students (I missed the chance to meet Natalie Portman, who graduated from the program a year earlier and could have been the love of my life), and Hillel, an organization that connects students to a pluralistic Judaism. My good English, as well as the experience I had working as a counselor at an American summer camp and my familiarity with the Jewish community, opened the program's doors for me. I did the job well, and a year later, was promoted on behalf of "Beit Hillel" to manage a series of meetings and lectures open to all students in the hopes of creating a fertile ground for brainstorming and creativity. This position was tailor-made for me: it required creativity and granted me a sense of freedom to take action and utilize my strengths. Among other things, I organized several meetings between students and authors, famous writers such as Eshkol Nevo and Yoram Kaniuk, as well as a series of films starring famous figures. The position at Hillel was another classic example of a win-win kind of program: the salary was admittedly low, but I gained many other things, like my own personal office at the university, which gave me a good base from which to get things done, and pivotal experience in motivating others without the authority granted by higher rank, like in the army, for example.

The ability to sway others into taking action is important in life, in every field – and university is a wonderful place to learn how to do it.

An equally important perk was getting to know Eylona, a social work major and an activist who led the Holocaust survivors' movement. I bid my roommates adieu and moved in with Eylona. We lived in one of Jerusalem's hardcore neighborhoods, in a very small yet equally charming studio apartment, on a narrow street packed with a ridiculous number of cats. To get to it, we had to cross the front yard of our kooky neighbor, Yaffah, who, unsurprisingly, was cat-obsessed. We ran our errands and did our shopping in the famous Mahaneh Yehudah open-air market nearby, way before it also became a thriving nightly hangout spot. As I flowed with the ebb of school and life, I also took on a position as a research assistant at the Truman Institute for Peace.

***

My time at university also came with a fair number of failures, like two unsuccessful attempts at getting into the esteemed and highly advantageous "Atidim" program. Not to speak of the Ministry of Foreign Affairs' cadette program, which never even bothered replying to my application. In the second year of school, I applied for a leadership fellowship at an organization called StandWithUs, a body that works in conjunction with the Ministry of Foreign Affairs to boost promising people with leadership potential in the field of public diplomacy. This was the inaugural year for the American organization's Israeli branch, and as someone who dreamed of becoming a diplomat (the dream of almost every political science and international relations student), its training program drew me in.

But unlike many of my friends who applied, I didn't get in. Oops. However, as often occurs, things eventually turned out for the best. Refusing to give up, I applied again the following year. This time, the admission process was more stringent, as the program was substantially more popular by then. Still, out of the 1,500 applicants, I was one of the elated 150 students who got accepted. It was my third year in school, and I was significantly more mature and ready for the program. Getting rejected the first time ended up being a blessing in disguise.

The program was incredibly thought-provoking. I got to meet talented people from different campuses across the country, and my social network grew exponentially. As part of the enrichment program, we attended various lectures by industry leaders and underwent various workshops focusing on important subjects such as public speaking. In addition, we initiated a project called Dialogue for Understanding, the goal of which was to connect Israeli students with volunteers from non-profits in the West Bank and East Jerusalem. Within the framework of the project, we wanted to close informational gaps we assumed the volunteers had due to both their lack of exposure to Israelis and their local media, which showed a very one-sided picture of things. We brought the volunteers to the university and established a series of meetings with students. As one of the project leaders, I was responsible for the external relations team, thus adding another skill to my resume.

Subsequently, I was chosen as one of the 15 lucky students who were sent to summer internships abroad at the organization's expense. At the end of my third year of studies, I flew with four other Israeli students – Dana, Asaf, Matan, and Ran – to London, and became an intern in the Public Diplomacy Department at the Israeli Embassy on Kensington Street. The ambassador at the time was the esteemed Ron Prosor, later to become Israel's ambassador to the United Nations.

I spent three months in London, where I stayed at the house of a Jewish family in West Hampstead, another incredible experience that suited the times. I learned quite a lot about British culture, which is far different than anything I'd been exposed to until then, and my time there included a few pub crawls and multiple afternoon teas (a custom I never grew to love and which I tend to practice only when I'm sick). At the London embassy, I met – for the first time, but not the last – Shimon Peres, Israel's president at the time who flew in for a visit. At a party hosted by a British family, I watched, along with other friends from the embassy, and wearing a blue Democratic party shirt, as Barak Obama made history and became America's first Black president.

One of the memories I carry with me from that time, which tends to surface whenever nostalgia kicks in, is a conversation I had with Ran and Matan at a local restaurant in Golders' Green, where we talked about life. Matan Nagola had just finished studying industrial engineering and management at the prestigious Technion University, and Ran Michaelis, who would later wed my friend Adi Balderman, studied political science, like me, but at a different school. Matan, who had a promising engineering career waiting ahead, as opposed to mine and Ran's uncertain fate, laughed at us for choosing to study something that didn't promise an actual income. We argued fervently, claiming that we were enjoying ourselves, studying things that interested us, and delving into side projects along the way. We assured him that we would, undoubtedly, make it.

And we were right. The three of us look back at that talk with fondness. Ran (who became the CEO of "Debate," a communications and management company, and later founded his own company) and I, probably earn more today than the average industrial engineer from the Technion. Equally important: we're both doing things we love that allow us to continue to flourish and create and not get stuck, in the comfortable position of having permanent employment and a stable income.

During my second year in school, I came across The Schusterman Foundation. Back then, I don't think I knew how to articulate it clearly, but today I can confidently state that one of the most crucial things when experiencing something new is immersing yourself in it, which is precisely what I did when I joined Schusterman, an organization that would play a very important role in my life.

Born in Tulsa Oklahoma, Charles Schusterman made his fortune from oil field exploration. In his words: "I ran into a lot of dry holes until one worked." The hole he found generated a lot of wealth, and he transferred about two billion dollars of it to the family foundation, which now works to strengthen youth with the aim of fostering positive change – for them, the Jewish community, and the entire world. The Schusterman Foundation works to realize its mission by cooperating with other organizations to advance high-quality education, leadership, and identity development, and it promotes various programs aimed at cultivating a sense of growth and leadership among young people.

Following Charles Schusterman's passing in 2000, his wife, Lynn, took over the family foundation. One of the articles published at the time expressed concerns about her competence to do the job. The headline read: "Is this woman ready for the job?" Lynn Schusterman likes to say that this is what gave her the motivation to prove who she is and catapult the family's philanthropic endeavors forward.

In 2007, the second ROI Summit was held in Jerusalem (ROI – Return on Investment, and also a word in Hebrew that translates to "my shepherd," the leader who ensures that nothing is missing). The purpose of this annual summit is to bring together 120 young Jewish entrepreneurs from Israel and around the world and put them through a one-week, eye-opening experience. Not only do they attend fascinating lectures, but they also cultivate global connections that have the potential to benefit the Jewish World and society as a whole. After the summit, participants become part of the ROI community and are eligible to receive annual micro-grants of $2,000 either for personal development or programs strengthening Israel or Jewish identity.

I came to this summit at just the right time – it hadn't yet gained the reputation it has today, and so it was a lot easier to get accepted. I got in thanks to my experience with StandWithUs and OneVoice. Today, now that the summit has grown immensely popular, these two programs would have never been enough to get me in. The fact that I was there when it all began not only opened doors for me, but granted me the opportunity to stand out and make an impact, which I, of course, went ahead and did.

It would have been easy to blend in with the crowd and get carried away by the summit, be just another one of 120 participants. But I saw the opportunity – an easily accessible community with a tremendous amount of resources – and decided it was better to be not just another one of 120, but *the one*. At the end of a pampering week at a nice hotel in Jerusalem – where we participated in empowerment workshops, heard lectures from entrepreneurs such as Shai Agassi, founder of "Better Place," which was then at the height of its glory, and rubbed shoulders while sipping on frothy cocktails – I made new friends.

I followed the logic of the stock market: the earlier you get yourself into something that isn't fully established yet, the chances to stand out are higher, and the added value is greater.

The risk is evidently higher as well, but so are the chances of hitting it big. What did I have to lose by attending ROI? Only a week of my life. In the worst-case scenario, I would have enjoyed myself, or not, and it would have ended there. But the chances of things taking off, as ended up happening, was much bigger. And so was the benefit.

The key is using the cards one is handed in life and capitalizing on them. You must use your time wisely, in a way that generates added value to you and the organization. For that to happen, it's important to map out what it is that you can bring to the table and invest in. For example, my added value, in any situation, is my ability to foster relations and bonds in order to stay on the radar, stand out and be impactful. I did so with OneVoice when I established the organization's first student chapter. And when the time came, I embarked on a tour in the U.S.

I stayed on ROI's radar as well: a year after the summit, I arranged a meetup in Israel, inviting all of the talented participants.

In 2010, when I was already a student at Harvard, I was invited to an ROI Summit, which included 120 selected members of the community from the first five years of the program. This summit was held – for the first and last time so far in its history – in Tel Aviv, as part of the city's centennial celebration. There, I met new friends who would later become some of my best ones, among them Shimon Levy, a former naval officer who worked at Birthright Israel and would later join me at the Kennedy School at Harvard, and Elad Shushan, a night owl who would go on to become a diplomat. Among the many activities the Summit offered was a party held on the roof of the Marina Hotel overlooking the sea. Without going into too much detail, let's just say that this was the last pool party hosted by ROI...

I'm a true believer in mixing business and pleasure. While bonds may form during formal work meetings, the real connections happen over alcohol and late-night hangouts. In the small hours of the night, when most people have left the party, discussions become far more intimate than those heard in office hallways, and they're the ones that stick with you over the years. One must view each experience as a whole, and this can happen only when you do what you enjoy with the people you like.

At this summit, I met Seth Cohen from Atlanta, who began working at the Schusterman Foundation as the Networks Director. Still figuring out his place, he was exploring how to build his role. Our relationship came at a point where he was relatively free to do many things with his position, and it benefited both me and the foundation greatly.

***

Accompanying all the experiences, organizations, communities, and volunteering activities I did over the years, were, of course, my studies. I enjoyed studying. I particularly remember courses on sports, politics, culture, and wars, and the courses on behavioral psychology. I derived a lot of pleasure from walking around campus, taking in the greenery, and meeting people along the way. I never complained too much about tests and got to enjoy the same accommodations I had as a high school student. Today, life is a lot easier for those with learning disabilities. I ended up with an average of 90.2 (out of 100) and was disappointed over failing to make the dean's list. At the end of the day, though, it didn't affect my future too much, and in any case, there's something nice about having what to strive for.

Despite having graduated, I still didn't know what I wanted to do in life. There was no definite path waiting for me to march on, but the experience and skills I accumulated over the years, in places where I stood for something I believed in, gave me an edge over others and opened plenty of doors. Looking back, I know that those years were utilized wisely, at times from a place of awareness, and others out of intuition. I seized opportunities that came along the way, and those experiences turned me into a great candidate for what was yet ahead. Each of my endeavors benefited my portfolio in one way or another: an internship in the Israeli Knesset contributed to my understanding of public policy; working with Hillel, StandWithUs and OneVoice fine-tuned my diplomacy skills; my time as a research assistant at the Truman Institute granted me both knowledge and a valuable recommendation letter from a leading researcher; and the ROI community, entrepreneurship and networking. Each experience added a different quality to my resume, and by the time I finished my undergrad studies, I had precisely what was needed to move forward.

During my time at the StandWithUs Fellowship, I met Jessica Atkins, a British woman who had moved to Israel to study at the Hebrew University. She offered me to be her replacement as a coordinator at the Friedrich Naumann Foundation – a German foundation with liberal views that supports human rights, the rule of law, and a prospering economy. The role – research assistant and event coordinator of the foundation – was perfect for me, both challenging and gratifying, offering various growth opportunities. Not to mention the nice salary: $1,700 per month for a part-time position, which at the time felt like a lot. I worked in the foundation's offices in East Jerusalem, which belonged to both the staff responsible for investments in Israel and the Palestinian Authority. Working at the foundation also granted me a glimpse of German culture, the most distinctive and strictest of cultures to which I'd been exposed to until then.

After two years together, Eylona gave me an ultimatum: either we get married, or we break up. I felt torn. While most of my friends back home were married (we were 26 by then), I knew I wasn't ready yet. On the other hand, I didn't want to break up. Things were going well for us overall. So I fled from the decision. I beg of you: don't set ultimatums in life, nothing good can come out of it. Everything has its time.

A childhood friend of mine, Yaron, was dealing with a similar situation. He was in the middle of his Ph.D. when he found himself at a difficult crossroads. One evening, we got together and spent the whole night deliberating on love and life. Eventually, we made similar choices.

One year earlier, I had applied for the Canadian "Sauvé Scholars" scholarship program, which seeks to empower young leaders around the world. Only 12 out of about 1,100 applicants were accepted and got to live in a mansion in Canada while studying at McGill University. Story of my life: I wasn't accepted, and my good friend Tomer was. While I dwelled on the rejection, he got to enjoy the perks of living in a mansion in Montreal. But I was determined to keep going, so I applied a year later, and a day after Eylona set that ultimatum, an email came in from Canada: I got accepted.

I chose Canada. The breakup was difficult, but it was the right thing to do. Like most of my ex-girlfriends, Eylona married the first guy she met after me. Three months after we broke up, I was in the mansion, and Eylona? Engaged. Both of us were happy.

My Word to the Wise

- When choosing where to study, ask yourself: do you want to be the head of the foxes or the tail of the lions? If you begin by being the lion's tail, you can work your way up and become a lion yourself. But where else can you go as the head of the fox?
- Another way to choose where to go to school: examine what else the place has to offer, other than the academics.
- You don't have to study medicine, engineering, physiotherapy, accounting, or social work. It's okay to study something that doesn't lead directly to a profession, as long as it sparks your curiosity and interest.
- Choosing where to study is a lot less dramatic than most people think. It's perfectly fine to stop and move on to something else.
- Universities and colleges are amusement parks, where each ride is an opportunity. You just need to dare, be bold, and hop on the right rides. Excelling in school isn't everything. It's better to stand out and create opportunities for yourself.
- Giving up isn't an option. Did you fail to pass the exams for a program or a job you really wanted? If it's important enough for you, try again. You might get accepted when you're more mature and ready.
- As you walk the path, equip yourself with a diverse enough resume that will open doors for you. Whatever you do – do your best.

A Word to the Wise from
Tomer Avital,
An Independent Journalist

The Art of Small Talk

I always found small talk boring, a waste of time. Over the years, I've managed to turn small talk into something of value. I discovered that it's possible to steer mundane talks to interesting places, and quite easily. Here are a few techniques:

Mystery – When you're confronted with ordinary questions like "What do you do?" or "Where are you from?" try and avoid one-word answers like "Hi-Tech" or "Jerusalem." Regular questions serve as the perfect opportunity to stand out. If I'm asked about my profession, for example, and I reply: "I work for a media outlet that ensures that elected officials are doing what's best for the public," it immediately ups the level of the conversation. As opposed to saying: "I work at X." People love mystery. Instead of saying, "I'm a software engineer at Expedia," you can entertain the listener with a riddle: "I work in a job where I change the way flight tickets are purchased." Or maybe even ask: "Can you guess?" From my experience, these answers spark a lot more enthusiasm and liveliness.

Cloaked Lists – We're all wired to uncover what we don't see in its entirety. What do I mean by that? If you want to talk about a place that matters to you, you can say: "City Hall is my second favorite place in town." In response, your partner will 100% of the time always ask about your first favorite place on the list. When that happens, you can easily steer the conversation to the topic you wanted to talk about in the first place. It's a bit sneaky, true, but it works just as well on romantic dates.

State Facts Instead of Questions – A good way to wake your partner up. Questions don't always work, especially with relatively quiet people. What can bring them to life is stating a fact, without a question mark at the end, particularly about something they're tied to emotionally. For example, to pry information from politicians who'd rather not speak to me, I swap questions for provocative statements. For example, "The law you passed has no chance," or "You will never become a minister that way." It's incredible to see how quickly they come to life and pour their hearts out.

Speak Passionately – Passion is one of the most memorable qualities. Whether it's about a volunteering project, a hobby, or a form of art you're enthusiastic about. Just listen to Yaniv talk about shared e-scooters... Notice that in every tacky Hollywood film, the hero has some bizarre hobby, like racing cars or fishing for catfish. Yes, it's fun to hear someone enjoy what they do – no matter what it is. That's why I tend to share my passions during small talk, for example, music, or the latest crisis

I encountered at work. The conversation instantly deepens and makes room for topics like emotions, which is far more interesting than everyday events. You can make this happen with a simple question: "And how did you feel about that?"

Failure Stories – People love hearing about other people's failures, it makes them feel better about themselves. The good aspect of sharing is that it encourages the other side to be vulnerable too. It takes the conversation to a deeper level in an instant. When I told my neighbor, whom I barely know, that I fought with my girlfriend, he suddenly opened up and let me in on some real hardships he was going through with his wife. It was a lot more fascinating and memorable than the talk we had about the building committee. This reminds me of another thing: I've spent the past few years giving hundreds of lectures about the media outlet I founded, but the most memorable responses I can recall came from "fuck up" nights, where people go on stage and share flop stories. I shared, for example, how a project of mine, in which I tried to keep tabs on lazy parliament members, failed. The crowd loved it and rushed to support my webpage straight after.

Switch It Up – Creativity doesn't necessarily mean developing some revolutionary, world-altering patent. You can be creative when constantly being forced into small talk. For example, instead of asking, "What do you do for a living?" ask for something deeper, "How do you spend your time?"

When We're Misunderstood – Frustrating, right? I've realized that the way out of it is to say: "I think I didn't explain myself well enough," instead of criticizing and mumbling, "You don't get it." Another example is the sentence "You're right," which you can replace with the more refreshing "I've never looked at it like that before," or encouraging comments like, "Don't stop now – I want to hear more!" "Makes sense, what else?" It will inject excitement and energy into the conversation.

When You Have Something Important to Say – Leave room for breathing space, and try to pause *before* saying something important, and *after*. It's amazing how the level of attentiveness will rise following these small breaks. Test it out with someone close. Come on, what are you waiting for?

CHAPTER 4

A Mansion in Canada
Meeting Bill Clinton

What can I say about the year I lived in a grand mansion along with twelve young leaders from around the world? The year Bill Clinton stared deep into my eyes; the year I co-founded a successful start-up, but lost millions along the way; the year my score was one of the lowest scores in the history of the GRE (a test required for graduate schools in North America) yet got into Harvard.

It was the year I went sledding, happily drunk, down a snowy mountain on New Year's Eve (and was nearly tossed into jail at the world's biggest winter carnival). The year I had a fuming argument about the Gaza flotilla raid – over a bowl of cornflakes, wearing nothing but my boxers – with the leader of the Green Party of Canada, and the year I learned how to properly hold a drink and have a relaxed conversation at cocktail parties. The year I was suspected of being sick with a dangerous and contagious disease and was thrown into confinement at a remote hospital in a developing country, ending the day in a fancy hotel, for the exact same reason.

How can I describe this year? Fantastic, well-timed, surprising, bizarre, revolutionary, all-embracing, eye-opening? Indeed, all of the above. Let's dive in.

***

The year began with a journey. My good friend, Tomer, had just returned from his stay at the Canadian mansion, and being as it was right before I was set to go do the same thing, we decided to get back on the road, knowing that we wouldn't have many other chances to travel freely together. In May of 2009, I flung my backpack over my shoulder and flew to South America. It had been three years since my first big trip abroad, and the time that had passed made these two adventures vastly different, despite their equal length (three months) and that they were on the same continent, one central, one south.

Equipped with experience and slightly more money, I knew it made no sense to be stingy with once-in-a-lifetime opportunities – for example, a trip to the Galapagos Islands. The money I'd save wouldn't amount to the experience I'd accrue. Of course, for each person, this depends on the timing and the place, as well as one's resources, yet I'd still recommend stopping and thinking before trudging the path of penny-pinching. It might pay to stray from your budget in favor of an exclusive experience or treat yourself to a higher standard of backpacking by taking a "loan" from your future paychecks.

Another thing I understood: You don't have to follow the herd and follow the road that has been traveled countless times. You don't even have to go on a long trip. It's not for everyone, and size really isn't all that matters. I'm a big fan of three-month trips; it's precisely enough time to open my mind, breathe some fresh air, and experience something new. Ask yourself what is right for you – at every point in life. Following the herd, or in our case, the "Israeli Hummus Trail," certainly won't make you an entrepreneur with innovative ideas.

Tomer and I had a blast on our trip. We met in Peru's capital, Lima, and headed up north near the city of Huaraz to enjoy the different treks the region offered. On our first hike, in a place called Laguna 69 – a beautiful lake surrounded by frosty mountains towering more than 15,000 feet above our heads – I struggled to acclimate to the height and puked my guts out. I enjoyed our second hike a lot more – the Cordillera Huayhuas, a mountainous region dubbed by National Geographic as the second most astonishing landscape in the world (after the Himalayas). Along with a group of young foreigners from around the world, I marched for eight days, accompanied by a local guide and donkeys that carried our bags over icy peaks, rapid rivers, scenic waterfalls, and crystalline lakes. At night, only the warm tea prepared by our guide managed to heat us up. From Cusco, we headed to the Inca Trail, an ancient pilgrimage that traverses dense rainforests and ends at Machu Pichu, the lost city of the Incas, whose captivating beauty makes the challenging trail worth it.

While in Peru, we volunteered in one of the village's

orphanages, a decision that suited Tomer and me, and which I highly recommend. Its great bonus, apart from a sense of accomplishment and contribution, is getting to know the locals. We helped with cleaning, cooking, and playing with the kids. Unlike me, who knew nothing more than *"Cuanto cuesta?"* and *"Por favor,"* Tomer spoke fluent Spanish, and ended up falling in love with another volunteer. We rolled with things. At the end of the day, these are the experiences that mold us into who we are.

One night, after meeting a local shaman, we journeyed to a village not far from Cusco to attend one of his mind-altering ceremonies. We didn't realize just how bizarre our experience was until two days later when the Shaman invited us to his daughter's wedding back in the village. It was only then that it dawned on us that the dozens of miles of the forest he led us around was actually just a few close yards. Don't blame us, we were just two geeks who spent long rides in open pickup trucks and chicken buses reciting words in English we learned from a book called "Vocabulary Builder." Even then I knew I'd take the GRE at one point.

On my final days in Cusco, I began coughing nonstop, and while COVID wasn't in the picture yet, I was still given concerned and irritated looks on the flight to Bolivia's capital, La Paz. I can't blame them. It really wasn't too pleasant sitting next to me. Upon landing, we were held up in passport control and told to wait. A moment later, a police officer arrived, announcing that I wouldn't be allowed into Bolivia but would instead be taken into isolation. By that point, I was in a complete haze. A loyal friend, Tomer accompanied me in the ambulance that drove us to a distant hospital, around 13 miles from the capital.

When we got off, we were met by a battery of reporters. One of them asked me how I was doing, but I was so nauseous that I had to step aside to vomit. All of this, of course, was being broadcast live. According to Tomer, the reporter stated, "A harsh sight indeed." We didn't really understand what was going on until we were told that I was the very first person in Bolivia sick with swine flu – a pandemic raging across the globe. While I would've given up the title of being the country's first plagued person, I loved having the story. A mere hour after landing in Bolivia, I was already on the evening news, and the following day, a picture of me – in a blue robe, my face covered with a mask – was plastered on the front page of the country's leading paper. The headline read: "Argentine Man Suspected as First Case of Swine Flu in Bolivia." Okay, so Israel isn't the only place where the media plays fast and loose with the facts. COVID, as a reminder, wasn't on anyone's radar at the time, nor did anyone dream of a day when the whole world would be under lockdown.

I spent two weeks in an isolated hospital room in the middle of nowhere, and every now and then, a nurse came to do some blood tests and take my temperature. While Israel's consul saw me on live TV and called saying he'd promise to help me, and I had my parent's support from Israel, and Tomer's support from La Paz, I still felt lonely and helpless, trapped in a situation I had no control over, condemned to adhere to other people's decisions over me. The nerdy "Vocabulary Builder" helped me pass the time, of which I had plenty. Thanks to those long days of isolation, I succeeded in expanding my English vocabulary. Apparently, one can find the light even in the darkest of times.

Two weeks in, my captors agreed to release me if I continued to self-isolate somewhere else – and that place was none other than the Ritz Carlton Hotel in La Paz, the only place with a doctor on site. As a lowly backpacker surviving on $7 a night, I found myself paying $150 for a room (Tomer was more than happy to be my roommate), but at least I was free to walk out to the lobby. After three weeks in that fancy hotel (to this day, my parents are still waiting for reimbursement for their travel insurance claim) the Bolivians were finally convinced that I wasn't sick with the swine flu and set me free. This event, which felt quite traumatic while it was happening, became – as most odd situations become – one of the most memorable experiences in my life. What's more, it's an awesome story to use in the game "two truths and a lie."

This less-than-stellar welcoming to La Paz convinced Tomer and me it was time to leave – immediately. So we set off on a rickety little plane, certain we would crash, and headed to the green entanglements of the jungles up north. We went on easy day hikes around the area and spent hours swinging lazily on hammocks protected by mosquito nets. After Bolivia, Tomer and I split up. He flew back home and I moved on to Argentina – to Bariloche, a city known for its chocolate – where I went on bike rides along Mendoza's vineyards, then to steakhouses and tango clubs in Buenos Aires, skydiving in Cordoba, and trekking on Argentina's Road of the Seven Lakes.

Throughout the whole trip, Tomer made sure to prepare me for my upcoming year in Canada. He described his time there as one full of opportunities – opportunities I'd probably never get again – and that I'd better make use of all that abundance.

Finally, I arrived in Montreal, nervous and excited, determined to use everything I'd learned to pave my way in Canada and make an impact on the world. Ambitious, yes, but not impossible.

Jeanne Mathilde Sauvé, the first woman to serve as the Governor General of Canada, founded the Sauvé Foundation for World Change. Each year, a promising and diverse group of around 12-14 young people from around the world – those who would one day spearhead social change, steer large organizations, and perhaps become heads of state – arrive at a grand mansion in Canada where they receive all the tools they need to become agents of social change. All of the applicants are below the age of 30, hold academic degrees, have valuable work experience, including a few proven achievements, and, most importantly, a dream they want to fulfill. In the mansion, under the most fruitful conditions imaginable and augmented by a prestigious scholarship, they are given the chance to nourish each other, attend any course of their choice at the nearby McGill University, and enjoy meetings with influential people from around the world. The program is viewed as a source of national pride in Canada, and its participants are sought-after guests at nearly every important conference in Montreal.

A freezing cold city with a special charm, Montreal is a fascinating blend of traditional European style with an American rhythm of life. It even has its own dishes, the most well-known being poutine, which some mistake for ordinary French fries. But don't be mistaken, these delicious potatoes covered in a cheese and-meat sauce are far from your average fries. We spent our first week in the beautiful city doing group seminars in the mountains and sleeping in tents on the banks of one of the city's many rivers. But despite the fantastic experience, we were all eager to get to the mansion.

Do you know that "home alone" feeling you get when you're left on your own while your parents fly abroad, leaving you to do whatever you want in the house (known or unbeknownst to them)? Well, imagine that scenario, but in a dreamy, five-story mansion in Montreal, with walls carved in wood and decorated glass windows, a decadent kitchen with a table fit for royalty, a lavish French-style living room with a chimney, and a massive library (the room was dauntingly beautiful, to the point where we were scared to enter it), lounge rooms, a sun terrace, a floor with a ping-pong table and a huge TV, illuminated workspaces, and a private room for each of us.

There are no duties in the house. A custodian polishes all the rooms, and the head janitor drops by daily to deliver Canada's local newspapers along with other international magazines. Each "scholar" is responsible for filling their schedule with all that is offered – conventions, tours around Canada and the U.S., meetings with leaders of different fields, workshops, courses, and other enrichment programs. All you had to do was grab what you wanted. You could wake up at noon and simply pass the time, or you could get up and take the day by storm. We appeared to sincerely want to change the world and were trusted not to waste this precious opportunity gifted to us. I liked the way Liran Gal, a 2007 graduate of the program, convinced Tomer to apply: "It gives you the space needed to disconnect from your daily endeavors," she said, "so you can contemplate, without any pressure, on a central question: what to do in life."

This was the first time in the history of the program that two Israelis were accepted. Along with me came Amnon Shefler, a pilot, and while the others cooked up dishes in the kitchen, we indulged in cereal and fried eggs.

In this magical mansion, I met people who would become my friends for life. Janet from South Africa, was a recipient of the prestigious Rhodes Scholarship for Advanced Studies at Oxford (whose recipients include Bill Clinton), and a representative of the former Apartheid nation. By the end of the year, she had come out of the closet. Years after the program, Amnon and I flew all the way to Cape Town to attend her wedding. There was Sarah Gonzales, a brilliant woman who was raised in several countries, among them Cuba and Spain, and had a master's degree from Oxford. Sarah would later cut off all ties with me and others, presumably because she had married Julian Assange, editor of the WikiLeaks website who disclosed classified documents and found refuge in Ecuador. Sarah and I enjoyed a short fling towards the end of the program, exploring and making proper use of the living room, like two kids stretching the limits. Shauntay, who came from west Canada, was a poet and author of children's books. James, a Brit in every sense of the word, was the founder of the first branch of the "Teach First" program, encouraging graduates to work as teachers. There was Mirwayze Nazet, a human rights activist who came from Afghanistan, Megan Carol, the American who had just completed her master's degree at Harvard, Maggie from Canada, who came from the field of sports and education and would later teach Inuits living in a remote village in northern Canada – an endeavor that would earn her the title of "Best Teacher in the World," one million dollars, and international esteem. There was Keith Stansky from the U.S. who was completing his doctorate at Oxford on historical warlords, Gabriel Burn-Lopez, the Canadian who founded a successful educational non-profit, and Eloge from Rwanda, a survivor of the civil war in which his father was slaughtered before his eyes. Eloge converted to Judaism during the program and was acquainted with Irwin Cotler, a former Canadian Minister of Justice and a fighter for human rights who is married to Ariela Cotler (an Israeli woman who served as a former Likud party secretary under former prime minister Menachem Begin). And, last but not least, Liam, a Canadian politician and law expert.

Each one of us got into the program with the help of recommendations and was asked to present an innovative project we would like to promote during our stay in Canada, with the use of all the tools provided in the program. My letters of recommendation came from Yaakov Margi, who by then was the Minister of Religious Affairs, and Daniel Lubetzky, the founder of OneVoice. As someone who was raised in a region of conflict, and due to the diplomatic experience I acquired in the Israeli embassy in London, as well as my time with the Hillel organization, I offered to build a type of toolbox that would allow embassies of conflict-stricken countries to present their nations in a different light and share the stories that aren't broadcast on the news.

A few years later, unrelated to my idea, Ido Aharoni, Israel's General Consul in New York, led a similar program with much success. Today, the fact that Israel is presented as the world's start-up nation, and Tel Aviv is known for its lively nightlife and progressive LGBTQ atmosphere, seems somewhat trivial. But a decade ago, Israel's reputation was mostly one of conflict and war.

Each one of us could choose a mentor to help guide us along the way, and I chose Jim Torczyner, a Jewish-Canadian from McGill University, who previously lectured at a university in Israel, and the man who founded the organization ICAN, The McGill Civil Society and Peacebuilding Middle East Program. We had long, in-depth conversations, some of them over a weekend at his lakeside home in Vermont, about building a peace program, looking beyond conflict, and aspects of education and empathy, which I believe are the basis and foundation of everything.

I'm a true proponent of mentors – inspiring figures who can help guide, advise, and cultivate you, all the more so if you can connect on a personal level. Don't hesitate to take advantage of the opportunity: look for the right mentors. Most people will be glad to hear that they are appreciated and will gladly contribute some of their knowledge and skills. I, myself, enjoy mentoring others and never turn down a request from someone in need of advice.

Communal life in the mansion gave way to profound, late-night conversations, which we referred to as "the vortex." The starring topics were civil war in Afghanistan, the Israeli-Palestinian conflict, and the Apartheid regime. One morning, I walked into the kitchen – still in a slumber and wearing only my boxers – where I came across Elizabeth May, a member of parliament and head of Canada's Green Party (then the country's fourth largest party). It was a few days after the Gaza flotilla raid, an event that shocked the world. Several Turkish ships had set course for the Gaza Strip, seeking to violate Israel's maritime blockade of the coastal enclave. One of the vessels, the Mavi Marmara, was raided by Israeli naval commandos. The event ended with nine casualties. Over a bowl of my favorite breakfast – a blend of cereals – I found myself fervently defending my country.

Meeting people from completely different cultures made me acknowledge the importance of having a global perspective on things. Cultivating this view, in the company of true friends from around the world, helped me perceive conflicts in a different light. It strengthened my vocation to stay in the U.S. and spread the Israeli story. I left the mansion with a resolve to show people the Israel that I know.

The Sauvé Foundation has managed to build such a good reputation that world leaders are happy to come and meet with the young scholars. This is how I found myself in front of America's former president, Bill Clinton, who looked me square in the eyes as he told me about his experience in the Golan Heights, where I grew up. This was my first time meeting someone who could really disarm you. He has a charming personality and a genuine knack for listening to someone as if what they're saying is the most interesting thing on the planet. Canadian Prime Minister Justin Trudeau, who we also met, has a similar charm, but Bill Clinton is on another level.

This was a year of intellectual stimulation. We studied French (I wasn't very good at it and managed to learn only one sentence – *"Je m'apelle Yaniv,"* "my name is Yaniv"). We rode our bikes to the university and took courses in business management and leadership, we rubbed shoulders with dignitaries who dropped by the mansion for cocktails and learned to efficiently present ourselves in a minute (also known as an "elevator pitch"). Dianne, Jeanne Sauvé's daughter-in-law, taught us etiquette and manners because she didn't want us to embarrass the family. Sitting at the head of the royal table, she showed us how to hold a fork, how to hold onto the same glass for the entire party, and most importantly, the golden rule: never come hungry to cocktail parties, because drooling over salmon tartars might come at the expense of landing an incredible opportunity. As someone who grew up in the Israeli countryside, I had a long way to go in terms of manners, and her course gave me some valuable tips for life.

Amnon and I used our Jewish roots to deepen our connections with the Jewish community in Montreal, as well as with two Jews who were loyal friends and board members of the program – Frederick Lowy, the president of Concordia University at the time (the second biggest in Montreal), and Harold "Sonny" Gordon, one of Canada's greatest lawyers. Gordon had a private box at hockey games and invited us all to watch the Montreal Canadiens play in a city where hockey is practically a religion.

The Jewish community in Montreal invited us on a lecture tour at "Hillel Houses" in Vancouver and Montreal, and before Jewish communities in other cities. We were also invited to celebrate the Jewish holidays with them. Amnon, Eloge, and I spoke with students from non-Jewish schools about Israel, and we read bits of the book written by Gilad Shalit, an Israeli soldier who was taken captive by Hamas. The Canadian Jewish News eventually dedicated a front-page article to me and Amnon. Toward the end of the year, we thanked the Jewish community for its hospitality in an appreciation event we held at the mansion. My Canadian grandmother (bubby) was also invited and enjoyed sipping alcohol as she listened to the kind words being said about her grandson.

We also knew how to have a good time. We enjoyed some "Big Brother" action, with all the perks the reality house offered, just without the cameras and eliminations. After all, we had a mansion all to ourselves. Janet taught us the wonders of South African beef, Amnon and I hosted Israeli nights of hummus and shakshuka, and James failed to get us into Marmite, that horrible British spread. We went on dates to Mount Royal, which overlooked our mansion, and enjoyed sledding in the freezing Montreal frost (minus 30 degrees Celsius on an average winter day) on New Year's. On Halloween, we hosted a crazy costume party on the balcony of the upper floor and invited everyone we knew.

Together, we watched the World Cup as it unfolded in South Africa and sang Shakira's "Waka Waka" at the top of our lungs. I kept "singing" it years later, on account of my notorious habit of getting stuck on a song until I find another one to replace it. On my 18th birthday, my friends threw a karaoke party for me in my backyard. What can I do, I love to make up words and sing nonsense... and who's to say the original words are better anyway? Well, my mom, for starters, who threatened to kick me out of the house if I didn't stop mangling lyrics to songs.

We drank Molson beer at the McGill pub and spent some time at my cousin's lakeside summer house. In February, we drove to the ice carnival in Quebec and stayed at the Hilton. We got into some trouble in the evening at a party after I instinctively elbowed a girl who pushed me. I didn't know she was a cop. She led me out in the freezing cold and ordered me to lay on the ice while I was wearing nothing but a T-shirt. Amnon, my loyal friend who came to my rescue, finished the night with a dislocated shoulder in a jail cell. I returned alone to my hotel room. We managed to get him out in the morning.

***

From the outset of the year in Canada, I had already made up my mind to get my master's in the U.S. and took advantage of the resources I had to send in the perfect application. Getting into schools in the U.S. is a lot more complex than how things work in Israel, where the only determining factor is your grades (a terrible system!). You need a lot of determination and motivation to push yourself forward, and you need to fine-tune your essay and the way you tell your life story to impress the people reading your application. This isn't something you can half-ass. You're navigating unknown territory because your acceptance doesn't rely solely on your grades, but on your life story, the way you articulate yourself, and your ability to impress those who go over your application. There's truly no way of knowing whether you'll get in.

I had Janet, who was great at writing essays, and Megan, a former student member of Harvard's acceptance committee, help me with my application and spent most of my free time tweaking it. They gave me valuable advice like focusing on creating a coherent storyline – growing up on a kibbutz and later the Golan Heights, my military service, advocating for peace – to ignite a sense of emotional attachment in the person reading my story. Keith and James suggested I beef up my application with numbers and statistics – how many people I managed, and how much money I raised on different occasions, for example. I walked around with a pocket full of words I had to learn for my GRE and asked each person I ran into to test me. Remember I mentioned that the university is an amusement park of opportunities? Well, the mansion in Canada was this amusement park's business class. It prepared me for Harvard because I took it in that direction.

The fact that I got a horrible score on my GRE – a confirmation of my poor aptitude for these kinds of tests

– didn't prevent me from applying to five top universities: Harvard, Columbia, the Hebrew University in Jerusalem, the University of Toronto, and Tufts University's Fletcher School of Law and Diplomacy. Luckily, top universities in North America look at applicants' files in a more holistic way, taking stock in particular of their leadership skills. I got into all of the universities except Columbia. There wasn't a real reason for my rejection (it's a lot harder to get into Harvard) but sometimes, all it takes is one person to read your application and turn it down. This is why you should never apply to just one place. Your file can land in the hands of a person who woke up on the wrong side of the bed, and that can be enough reason for them to shatter your dreams.

There's another reason you should apply to several places: if you get into numerous institutions (or workplaces), you can play your cards better. When I told Fletcher that I got into Harvard, they offered me a $20,000 scholarship for me to attend their school.

But I wanted Harvard, and to this day, everyone from the program remembers my roar of joy that rang throughout the mansion, from the cellar to the fifth floor, when the email with the good news arrived. I doubt I could have done it without my loyal friends from Canada, and their partnership made it so they were just as happy as I was about it. Now, only one problem was left: I needed $100,000 to fund those two years at Harvard.

Getting a scholarship is a long and draining process. It requires a lot of research, deliberation, investment, help from others, and a whole lot of optimism and patience.

You shouldn't overlook any of these stages – from searching for the right scholarship to applying for it.

Additional tips: search online for scholarships, and look into each one, even those that appear irrelevant – you never know what might come of it. The same goes with your resume: highlight your "x-factor." Market yourself efficiently, look for the right people to write recommendation letters for you, and make sure they come from diverse backgrounds. Make sure to polish your application time and time again, ask people from different fields to help, and listen to their advice. Don't lose hope, even after getting rejected – all you need is one positive answer.

I applied for several scholarships, among them, the E. David Fischman Scholarship, awarded by the Jewish community in St. Paul, Minnesota. It was originally intended for Israelis pursuing doctorate degrees in law, political science, or economics at any of the Ivy League schools. However, Eli Novershtern, who would later become a good friend of mine, was the pioneer who managed to convince the foundation to open the scholarship to students doing their master's degrees – proof that we should never give up on creating change, both for ourselves and others, and we should never assume something is a foregone conclusion.

Members of the foundation suggested we do the interview online, but I decided to take advantage of the fact that I was in Montreal and bought a $480 airline ticket to Minnesota in order to maximize my chances of winning the Harvard scholarship. I paid and flew over to frigid Minnesota, where I stayed in a cheap motel – all this for a one-hour interview, but an in-person one with the scholarship director, Dan Mogulson. He appreciated the fact that I traveled all the way to see him and reminds me of it each time we meet. With all due respect to Zoom (then Webex), there's nothing like face-to-face interaction. When you have so many competitors, either for a job or a scholarship, every little advantage, even a bit more effort from your end, can make the difference. As my dear friend Alex Banayan says, there is always a "Third Door," which he made in to a bestselling book that I highly recommend reading.

I left the interview feeling good. I knew I did the best I could and tried my hardest to nail it. A few weeks later, I received a positive answer. I had gotten full funding for my studies (I ended up paying $500 and got back $100,000, a return of 200 times the initial investment) – a classic example of treating life as a "start-up," which most people don't do.

Even if I wouldn't have received the scholarship, I still wouldn't have given up on my dream. Perhaps I would have taken out loans to achieve it. But this scholarship surely made fulfilling this dream a lot easier.

***

At the height of my work on the original project for the Sauvé Program – the toolbox for countries in conflict – an enticing opportunity came my way. Amnon told me that his brother Yuval was helping out at a newly born start-up called "Comtribute," which was looking to onboard someone to help launch operations in its main market,

North America. It was a start-up founded by two Israelis who had worked for Amdocs and Microsoft and developed a free product (in the form of a toolbar), meant to help non-profits raise money, stay in contact with their donors, and build a community. In addition to enhancing the sense of communal commitment in those who use the toolbar, each search done with it yields three cents for the organization (this was the heyday of computer toolbars, which have long been extinct. Goes to show how fast technology evolves).

I loved the idea. Yuval connected me with Nadav Bernshteter, one of the founders, a cool redhead with a ton of experience (who would later reveal how frustrated he was after our first conversation in which he felt like I didn't understand a thing). He didn't get why I was introduced to him, but after a few talks, he realized I was picking up on things, and entrusted me with the role of establishing sales operations for North America.

This line of work was foreign to me – I'd never joined a start-up before, nor did I have experience in the tech sector, but I knew how to sell. And, as mentioned before, I'm a fast learner. I knew this was a once-in-a-lifetime opportunity to create change, and, admittedly, a good business deal – joining a brand new company, receiving compensation, and building my reputation, all during my year of limitless opportunities in Canada.

First, I presented my Social Impact Initiative. I explained to the leaders of the Sauvé program that I fully believed it to be a venture that would help the world. I convinced them it deserved a spot among the projects of the prestigious program, in the hopes that they would allow me to work on it instead of my initial proposal and even help me out. I knew this was a great chance to capitalize on the situation and leverage it.

Knowing that there was nothing to lose, and everything to gain, I was full of anticipation. Due to the program's prestige and the leaders involved, I knew I had all the tools and resources a new entrepreneur could only dream of. The people I met were leaders in their fields and they perceived me in the same manner. I took advantage of my position. I held a press conference in the mansion, funded by Sauvé. I appeared in the biggest Canadian and international newspapers such as The Gazette and USA Today, photographed in the lavish living room of the castle, presenting "Comtribute" to the world.

It was easy to connect with a project that helps non-profits raise money for worthy causes. And to convince people to do so, I used the age-old cliché "fake it till you make it" and made a lot of noise when I managed to get huge names on board – large organizations like the WWF (World Wildlife Fund), after which came others, among them, OneVoice, whom I had known before. When you're just starting out, it's best to contact sources you're familiar with. My biggest advantage was that I was in the right place to do so, in a mansion where CEOs of large organizations eagerly rushed, and I had no shame whatsoever to lecture them about this important project. I sold it by emphasizing why it was crucial to develop such a tool now, and why it was right for the world. Sauvé's reputation was my stamp of legitimacy.

Nadav was stunned by the success. I, myself, was still dwelling over the fascinating blend of Social Impact, which, up until that point, didn't exist in Israel, and would later become my thesis topic at Harvard. Eventually, out of the 13 residents of the mansion, my project saw the most success, both in terms of realizing its potential and exposure.

All this happened because I wasn't afraid to veer off my original plan. Normally, we find it easier to stick with what we intended in the first place and end up ignoring other opportunities that pop up along the way. To my delight, I was in the right place at the right time, which allowed me to connect with my passion and dare to do something else. Don't be afraid to be opportunistic at times. This was an opportunity to learn and acquire a new set of skills that would take me a step further in life. I managed to create a job while still in the program, which both provided me with a solid income and took me to places I'd never have reached otherwise. I made a lot of mistakes in the business and start-up world, but to my credit, I learned from each one of them.

Following Comtribute's success, I wanted to postpone Harvard for a year, but the Fischman Foundation refused to put a hold on my scholarship. I was faced with a serious dilemma: stay with the company I helped grow that was just now spreading its wings (under the assumption that profits would keep rising), or give up a $100,000 scholarship? Eventually, I chose Harvard. Despite wanting to stay with the company, I believed that Harvard, all the more on a full ride, was a much bigger opportunity in the long run.

I didn't know then that I was going to lose out on millions. While I went to Harvard, Comtribute changed course. It grew and made massive amounts of money. The nagging thought of losing out crept up at times, but today, I don't regret my decision, not for a second. Harvard was waiting for me, and choosing it was just the right ticket to ride.

My Word to the Wise

- Find the right path for you – following the herd won't turn you into an entrepreneur who does things differently.
- Search for unique programs around the world that can provide growth opportunities and the development of a global perspective. Only outside of your country, outside of your comfort zone, can you understand where you came from, and where you're heading.
- With the help of scholarships, you can study anywhere in the world. All you need to do is search for those fitting your attributes. Invest time looking for one – it's strenuous, yet worth it.
- Learn how to present yourself concisely in a way that will impress those listening and teach them all about your strengths.

A Word to the Wise from
Lana Zaher,
Partner at "Al-Arz" Tahini

*"Go with your gut feeling,
even if it means taking risks"*

When we look at business owners, we may sometimes be astonished by the choices they make, but that's because we haven't taken into account the things they've been through to get there. My father, who previously worked as an electric motor engineer, established our family factory, producing high-quality tahini, in a spur-of-the-moment decision in 1990 in Nazareth. He developed the machinery and opened a small company. Naturally, my brother and I grew into the business.

In 2003, my father passed away suddenly. My mother, who up until then was a schoolteacher, didn't want to give up the family business, so she took it upon herself to carry on the torch. She recruited the workers and learned everything from scratch – every cog in every machine, which suppliers to contact, and which banks to approach. She certainly broke the glass ceiling.

It was a period of recession, and I was just 19 years old and in my first semester of school. The truth is that I wanted to work in diplomacy. For years, I feared committing myself 100% to the family business. I was scared to ruin what my parents had worked so hard to build. At the beginning of my studies, I would drop by the factory only twice a week. Even then, I'd always find something else to do. Despite knowing that I would be a significant part of the family enterprise, I struggled to take responsibility.

Gradually, I realized how different it was to join an already existing company, rather than build one from scratch. When you work with a blank slate, you can set the tone and carve your own motto, but when you join an already running machine, you need to find common ground with those around you, which is not always easy. When joining a business, particularly a family business, it's crucial to define specific roles and separate the professional from the personal. It's important to create a solid, winning team, and fill positions based on people's skills and experience.

As the next generation of my family's business, I felt a huge responsibility, because apart from my family's expectations to give it my all (at times, too much), there was a sense of hope that the new generation would take the business – cautiously and with reverence to everything that had been accomplished – to new heights. I've often contemplated the delicate task of letting my ideas shine without ruining what exists.

Once I started enjoying myself, I knew I was in the right place. I developed, created, and pushed for innovative ideas, fully believing in what our product has to offer. Today, I am constantly learning, making sure to listen to my intuition while daring to ask others for advice. I came to understand that when running a business, there's no room for ego, only open-mindedness, learning, and understanding that it's okay to make mistakes.

In fact, that is the only way to reach the goals we've set for ourselves.

Self-fulfillment came from an unexpected place. After taking the world by storm with our brand, it was a small event here in Israel that filled me with pride. We decided to donate to a hotline assisting Arabs from the LGBTQ community. For us, it was a simple and reasonable move, but this donation created havoc among clients, some of whom have boycotted us to this day. In one fell swoop, a substantial amount of our target audience was gone, just for standing up for what we believed in. But on the flip side, the wave of hatred we experienced was counter-balanced by a giant wave of love and appreciation by people from Israel and around the world, and our relatively modest donation became an international story that got people talking. Members of the Arab LGBTQ community finally got the recognition they deserved.

Being able to impact society through our brand was the most satisfying feeling I'd ever felt. Promoting social change with such a simple act moved me more than any business deal I landed. I guess my advice for you is to go with your gut feeling, with what you enjoy, even if that means taking risks. A genuine desire to impact the world is what leads to success.

CHAPTER 5

Harvard

And how I missed out on
a dreamy trip to China

In my early days at Harvard, I occasionally felt the need to pinch myself: Is this real? Am I really here, Yaniv Rivlin from the small town of Katzrin, in this American sanctuary of knowledge? My presumption coming to Boston was that everyone around me was smarter. I mean, they were Harvard students, and I was probably here by mistake. Classic imposter syndrome. However, I shed this thought about halfway through my studies and started feeling worthy of my place on campus, largely due to the positive reinforcement coming from the people around me.

Let's put things on the table: I wasn't a straight-A student. There's a common phrase in Harvard: "B's get degrees," meaning, even if you got a B, not an A, you still get a degree, which is true. In America, you normally fight for good grades during your undergraduate studies, presumably because you're younger, and with young age comes fervent competitiveness. But also, because those grades might be your ticket into a coveted grad school. But as a grad student, you no longer have to strive for excellence. There's not much difference between an "A" and a "B," especially when you go to Harvard or any other prestigious university, which gives you enough prestige and doesn't really require that you put in more effort, unless you're planning on doing a Ph.D. The student's goal is to learn, broaden their knowledge and finish their courses on a good note, which aligns with Harvard's goal of ensuring that the students who've managed to get in won't fail. Very few students fail to graduate.

Along with the understanding that I didn't have to excel, I quickly sensed that, unlike my undergraduate experience, at Harvard, I wanted to devote myself fully to the student experience. In America, as opposed to Israel, it didn't seem common to work while studying – there didn't seem to be part-time jobs fit for students. Students seemed to attach great importance to their expensive studies and invest in them. I knew I was experiencing something that wouldn't come around again and that I should get as much as I could from it. In truth, the hefty price tag was looming above my head as well, even though I paid for it with a scholarship.

And anyway, the way the program is built doesn't leave much time for anything else. Most classes have mandatory attendance and are not taught in huge halls with three-hundred students crammed inside. Discussions are done in small, intimate classes, and require that the students pay close attention to projects and tasks that are carefully looked at. A big part of these classes involves case studies and actual research projects, which stimulate the students' thought processes and improve their ability to deepen their knowledge instead of simply reciting the course material. The students are required to come to class with an understanding of what they're being taught, and a solution for problems probed by the professor, who will always try to challenge them. Whoever doesn't come prepared is already behind.

Nevertheless, throughout those two years at Harvard, I managed to achieve much more than I ever dreamed of and conquered new heights.

***

I fell in love with Harvard practically from the get-go. It's impossible not to. On every corner, the Charles River can be seen flowing through Massachusetts, separating Boston from Cambridge, the student town housing of Harvard, Tufts, and MIT. Nearly everywhere in the vicinity, largely due to the red-bricked buildings radiating grandeur, the chronicles of history permeate the air. The fact that practically every president of the United States studied there certainly adds to the sense of reverence.

In the center of Harvard Yard is the famous statue of John Harvard, one of the university's first benefactors. Tourists enjoy taking pictures by his side, unaware that first-year students are asked to pee on him as part of their initiation ceremony. Many undergrads make a living by guiding tours across the university's various schools to Harvard Square, which serves as a sort of pilgrimage site. Tours brimming with historical tidbits.

Of all the things Cambridge has to offer, I was actually drawn to bars like Kong, located above a repugnant Chinese restaurant, where we would finish the night by calling: "To the Kong!" God only knows why that bar became our usual hangout spot.

My first dilemma at Harvard was where to live: rent an apartment, or find a room at Harvard housing, a type of dormitory, but at a higher standard than we're accustomed to in Israel. I ended up choosing the dorm, because I had too many things to adjust to and wanted to take the housing dilemma off my mind. The experience of living in a dorm and getting to know new people was a huge bonus and is certainly recommended, at least during one's freshman year.

I chose my roommate in advance – Josh Martin, whom I'd met at the ROI Summit in Israel. Even though he came from Newton (a Boston suburb), Josh preferred to live in a dorm. We were lucky enough to get an apartment with a view of the Charles River on the 21st floor of Peabody Terrace, a dormitory that was considered the pinnacle of luxury in the 1970s and won an architecture award due to its efficient construction. If it was up to me, though, I wouldn't have given that prize to someone who decided that the only elevator should stop every third floor[3] – it made moving into the place a nightmare. One of the main advantages of living in a dorm was my neighbor from the 20th floor – Dany Bachar from Venezuela, a Zionist who went to Hebrew University in Jerusalem. He

---

3. Yes, the elevator started on 1, and didn't stop on the 21st floor where I lived, which meant that I had to go to the 22nd floor and walk everything down one flight.

helped me with statistics, which I found terribly difficult. The dorms were a ten-minute walk from Harvard's Kennedy School, the school of public policy and government I attended. Not a walk in the park when Boston's winter hits, but it could have been worse.

Harvard welcomes its students with a week-long initiation, beckoning: You are wanted here, and from now on – and hopefully for the rest of your lives – you will be an inseparable part of this place and its tradition. In the opening lecture by the head of the alumni department, where she informed us of what we were to expect, as well as the perks the university had to offer, she asked which of the students was single. All of the bachelors and bachelorettes got on their feet. Even if this was meant to be a light-hearted joke, it gave the impression that Harvard would be glad to bring people together for life. After all, if you marry someone you met at Harvard, the sense of belonging to the place skyrockets. In fact, a generous number of couples came out of my year. There you have it, another good reason to come to Harvard. In that first meeting, we received a water bottle, courtesy of Harvard's alumni association. Yet another symbol of belonging; simple yet significant.

Throughout the initiation week, each student got an opportunity to present themselves. I particularly remember a Korean astronaut, an Ethiopian minister, and someone who carried on the matchmaking theme and gave out his number. Apart from myself, there was another Israeli student – Yael Bar Tur. The track we studied was far less popular for Israelis than the track for people in the middle of their career, who were eligible to receive scholarships from the Wexner Foundation. The Wexner program is intended for people aged thirty and above, so I couldn't be considered for it. "Wexner people" come with remarkably diverse work experience, among them retired chiefs of staff and former parliament members.

One student who arrived at Harvard in 2013 was Moshe Kahlon, who would later become Israel's minister of communication and successfully implemented well-received reforms in the cellular phone market. Kahlon attended an eight-week executive course. Right off the bat, he realized his English wasn't good enough and that he needed to find a creative solution to survive. He e-mailed the Israeli consulate requesting help in finding an Israeli student to help him overcome his language issues. I had a few friends who stupidly declined the request, but one person who did appreciate the magnitude of the opportunity was Roy Folkman, who was a Wexner fellow due to his work in the public sector in Jerusalem. Kahlon and Folkman would go on to become friends, which eventually led to Folkman's appointment as chairman of the Kulanu political party that Kahlon formed upon his return from Harvard. Folkman was elected to the Israeli Knesset on the party's ticket and was Kahlon's right-hand man during his tenure as communication minister. It just goes to show how important it is to capitalize on opportunities.

Initiation week was fascinating. Apart from getting to know the ins and outs of this influential place, I felt wanted, part of something big. The message transmitted to us was: we are here for our students, for them to have an experience. Unfortunately, most academic institutions in Israel don't show as much interest in their students, therefore they lose them right after graduation. Unlike America, Israel doesn't try to instill in their students a sense of belonging, loyalty, and tradition, which, in America, manifests in the alumni's sense of commitment to the well-being of the school that provided them with their education. When I attended the Hebrew University, the alumni's association was a neglected afterthought. Only years later did it become slightly more significant. Today, that has changed, and I serve as a member of its advisory board, out of a firm belief that such an association is crucial for the student's overall experience. Higher education, should, in my opinion, be a holistic experience, and it's important to create that sense of belonging the moment the students step through the university gates, one that will carry on after graduation.

The first year at Kennedy involves mainly mandatory courses. One of the reasons I wanted to go to this school is because of its multidisciplinary approach, and its macro view of things. Their courses touch on many different subjects, stemming from a firm belief that to serve society adequately, one must be knowledgeable in many fields.

The elective courses, which comprise most of the second year, are elected via the points system: students distribute their points between the different courses they would like to take. I put my chips on a course taught by Professor Ron Heifetz – a doctor, surgeon, psychiatrist, cello player, and professor of public policies who is seen as a guru in the field of leadership. His course on adaptive leadership, predicated on many people acting to affect broad-based systematic change, is one of two courses at Harvard that students, even 20 years after graduating, rate as having affected them the most.

Heifetz integrates psychological theories into procedures of decision-making and leadership. He developed a school of adaptive leadership, causing those who study with him to view their leadership through a different lens. The course works in the following way: students divide themselves into small groups, and each week, one member of the group presents a behavioral-leadership challenge one might face. A discussion plays out in the following format: representation of the dilemma, time for questions without responses, additional clarifying questions, discussion, and recommendations. The objective is to find additional ways of looking at the challenge through Prof. Heifetz's framework. During the lesson, one group presents the class with their dilemma, and the discussion plays out under the same guidelines. On one occasion, the student presenting the dilemma was Ethiopia's defense minister.

Heifetz's techniques and strategies helped me along the course of my career, particularly his tip to take a step back and look at things from a different perspective, or in his words: "Take a step from the dance floor to the balcony."

The diversity of Kennedy's elective courses is a reflection of its distinguished student body. Harvard in general, and the John F. Kennedy School in particular, has one of the most diverse demographics in America, its students coming from distinctively different places across the globe. Students of the Kennedy School are normally older than those studying law or business management – the average age is 28, the age I attended Harvard – and they come from the world of business, public service, and diplomacy. This concoction, infused with the experience of 250 students, allows for an expansive learning experience with a broader perspective on burning topics.

HKS offers far more than its exceptional courses. The lecturers are often preceded by their own reputations – for example, Prof. Robert Putnam, a political scientist who teaches about social capital and social unity, and Prof. Lawrence Summers, Harvard's former president who once served as the U.S. secretary of the treasury. Moreover, the "Fellows" of Harvard, who come from different institutions across the globe, are obliged to teach in small classes. They are eager to connect with the students and strive for a reciprocal gain of wisdom. The overall ambiance of the place dismantles any sense of stringent hierarchy. All students need to do is choose from this immense pool of wealth offered to them.

This wealth includes lectures by world leaders – presidents, prime ministers, Nobel prize winners – in a hall called "the forum," a large room located in the center of the school. As students, it became almost trivial sitting in the forum with our laptops, typing away notes delivered by Bill Gates, John Kerry, Hillary Clinton, Malala Yousafzai, as well as Ehud Barak (Israel's former prime minister).

During the Arab Spring, protests raging in Cairo's Tahrir Square were broadcast on a large screen in the middle of the school, and students from around the world watched together. Cries of joy reverberated from the screen, cheering on what seemed like, at the time, a true revolution in the Islamic world.

Speaking of the Arab Spring, one of the beautiful things about Harvard is its incredibly fast response to global events. As the situation in Egypt boiled over, Harvard opened a course about the Arab Spring, taught by American journalist David Ignatius, who covers the Middle East for the Washington Post. Each week, the course dealt with another country, and in nearly every lesson, a different guest lecturer would drop by, such as Ben Rhodes, Deputy Head of the National Security Council in the U.S. under President Obama. In addition, the students were divided into pairs, and each was assigned a country they would research and then present their findings to the class. I had the somewhat surreal experience of being paired with the prince of Qatar, Mohamad Al Thani, and together, we needed to discuss Syria, my childhood neighbor to the north. It was fascinating to learn about historical events at a time when history was very much in the making. In retrospect, everything turned out to be the exact opposite of what was expected: Egypt was then the pinnacle of hope, Tunisia was in a horrific state, and no one expected a vicious civil war to break out in Syria. Conclusion? Even the greatest experts can't definitively predict what lies ahead.

***

Harvard's Kennedy School is a very progressive place that strives to promote liberal values – the topic of human rights is prominent – very much in line with my worldview. Inevitably, however, discussions would arise about Israel and Palestine and, overall, foreign news outlets shed a very different light on the country, vastly different from how I view the "real" Israel. Thus, my desire to show people other sides of the country significantly grew during my time abroad, beginning in the Sauvé program and extending to Harvard.

Along with Wexner fellow Yishay Sorek, I was chosen as head of the Israeli chapter at the Kennedy School. We began arranging different events on campus, like Israeli wine nights with bottles from wineries from the Golan Heights. Harvard is a magnet for businessmen and women, and an evening to get people drunk is always a hit, surely with a glass of great Israeli wine. But the pinnacle of our events, which I will always be proud of, is arranging the "Israeli Trek" and the "Israel Conference." At the end of that trek, I came to the realization that I was truly a fit for Harvard.

Every year, on spring break, Kennedy students arrange trips in their countries in an attempt to show their landscapes and deepen people's familiarity with the culture. Students need to choose between a trek in China, Korea, or Germany – a small example of the vast number of choices they have. We decided to expand this tradition, which had begun two years earlier, and put Israel on the map in order to show them the "true Israel." Remember that diplomatic toolbox I came up with in Canada but never materialized? At Harvard, it came together in a different form, no less meaningful. The passion that flowed through my veins, which was now more cohesive, manifested in a well-planned and carefully built trip to Israel, my dear country.

The first stage was getting donations to help fund the exquisite journey we were planning. We didn't know what we were getting ourselves into, and good thing we didn't, because if we would've known that raising donations from philanthropists and formulating a complete itinerary was a full-time job, we probably wouldn't have had the guts to do so. Fortunately, there is no shortage of rich, Jewish Harvard graduates who feel committed to giving back. We managed to come into contact with two remarkable alums – billionaires Jonathan Jacobson and Seth Klarman. On a Friday morning, Yael Bar Tur and I showed up at Seth's office in Boston, located on the 50th floor of a magnificent building, eager to give him our pitch. A short while later, we walked out with a check for $25,000, signed and ready. Wow! While we hoped to get a donation from him, we never imagined ourselves walking out of that very meeting with a check in hand. We walked to a nearby park, looked at each other in disbelief, and uttered: "So that's how you do business in America?" We then grabbed a drink at the same pub where the sitcom "Cheers" was filmed. Jacobson ended up donating a similar amount. We were good to go.

We easily managed to lure students from the U.S., Peru, Korea, Mexico, and other countries to join our trek and fill a whole bus. There was even a waiting list. To folks studying at HKS, Israel and its neighbors feel pretty exotic. Each hummus night, and during brief hallway chats, we would promise them a fair and representative display of the country: touching upon the political situation, while enjoying what the place has to offer – and we meant every word of it. After overcoming complex logistical hurdles, we managed to put together a spectacular journey.

I believe in soft landings, which is just how we did it in March 2011, at the height of Israel's Purim festivities, smack in the middle of the outlandish costume parties of Tel Aviv, the coolest city in the world. It's easy to connect with the place, and easier when you're hanging out with a group of friends, drunk and in togas, roaming a street party. It's also easier to connect with a city when you're going to the best clubs and each one welcomes you with a sign that reads "Welcome Harvard" – a little something my good friend Elad arranged, then a serious party organizer and today a diplomat.

We hung out non-stop, barely slept, and showed up to each of our scheduled meetings yawning and droopy-eyed.

But with all due respect to Tel Aviv, we didn't come to Israel just to have fun.

We continued to the visitor center of "Better Place," a company that was once the exemplar of the "Start-up Nation." As someone who grew up in the north of Israel, I dragged everyone to the Golan Heights, and from the summit of Mount Bental, we oversaw the Syrian border on one side and the Lebanese border on the other. If the former high-ranking U.S. army veteran in the group got excited over the borders, others were moved by the Sea of Galilee – where Jesus walked on water. There's no better place than Israel to create a holistic experience – a small patch of land full of history and complexity that can be traced in a week.

During our trip, we drove from the Dead Sea to Jerusalem to meet with the late President Shimon Peres; Reuven Rivlin, then the Speaker of the Knesset; Stanley Fischer, then governor of the Bank of Israel; and with Supreme Court Justice Salim Jubran, who spoke about Israel's judicial system, which included his point of view as an Arab judge who made his way to the top. The Harvard halo surrounding us helped set up all these encounters. I used my connections to arrange a meeting over some beer with fellows from StandWithUs.

If we would've ignored the Palestinian Authority, we would've failed to do our job properly.

Thus, we went to Ramallah to meet with Saeb Erekat, a former member of the Palestinian Legislative Council and the Palestinian Authority's chief negotiator with Israel.

The trip to Israel was an amazing experience for everyone who participated, myself included as the host and organizer. It was moving to show Israel from my point of view, to "sell" it to others (sales skills can be applied even when it comes to countries) and see them indulge in the new experience, creating a heightened sense of pride for my country. I believe that there's no better diplomacy than seeing things with your own eyes, meeting people in person, and using your senses to experience things to the fullest. If you want to understand the real situation in a country and gain a new perspective, you must step in and see for yourself. During our bus rides, insightful discussions arose. For example, on one occasion, the former American general confessed in my ear: "After standing on Mount Bental, I now understand why Israel can't give up the Golan Heights" (and this was before the civil war in Syria erupted). Another friend, Keith, came to me after the Purim street party and exclaimed, "Israel blew my mind. This isn't how I thought it would be." Over time, many of these people held senior roles such as congressmen and senators, and the fact that they'd visited Israel, at such a critical point in their lives, is priceless.

We came back from the trip on a high. I realized that I love arranging these sorts of things and that I was good at it – creating the experience and interaction, accompanying people as they come out different than how they started, and arranging something that bears fruit within a relatively short period of time. In fact, this was a genuine entrepreneurial process. I returned to Kennedy with 50 people who felt like they owed me for providing such a rich and distinct experience. This isn't to say that they all became Israel's number-one fans, but I do know that they certainly came back with an open mind and an understanding that the situation is way more complex than they thought.

It was the first trip I'd arranged to Israel, and over the course of my career I'd do it again, but on a larger scale. We were the first to identify the potential of this journey. When they understood what we did and how it changed the perspective of the world's future leaders, an organization called Israel & Co was founded, specializing in arranging hundreds of trips like these every year. To this day, I have a close connection to this important organization and speak with their student treks (I've spoken to more than five of their groups just this past year).

One of the things that weighed on the journey was Israel's stringent entrance process. Many of the participants had to go through intensive questioning on their way in and out. Natalia, from Ukraine, had her laptop confiscated, and another, an Amnesty activist, was denied entry to the county. Nothing helped, not even the intervention of Ophir Pines, a Kennedy graduate and Israel's former minister of the interior. While I understand Israel's need for security, and consequently the inquiries and strict entry requirements, they don't exactly help those trying to show others a different side to the country. Despite the difficulties, the trip I arranged in my second year at Harvard was in even greater demand. I, myself, paid a high price for the trip's success by experiencing FOMO for missing out on the trek to China organized by my good friend, the son of a senior member of the Chinese communist party. My friend arranged an incredible journey to his country, which included luxurious experiences and taking part in fascinating meetups. I couldn't join that trip because I was busy arranging the one to Israel, but he promised me my very own tour later on. In the meantime, however, as part of a political plot, his mom was accused of murder and his dad of corruption. His house in Boston was besieged by the media. Even I had to deflect CNN reporters as they tried to interview me about my good friend. Somehow, through his remarkable perseverance, he managed to graduate. To this day,

I'm waiting for that private tour he promised me, but it likely won't happen anytime soon.

In our second year at Harvard, competition arose: the Palestinian trek. Its organizers arranged a pretty one-sided view of things, showcasing the occupation in all its glory, or better put: lack of glory. It's hard to blame them, but if I were in their shoes, I wouldn't have built it that way. Unlike the Israeli trek, this one wasn't much fun. However, many of its participants came back from it pro-Palestinian after meeting so many people whose houses were demolished. We could have also shown similar images on the Israeli side but decided to take a different and more nuanced route.

But what worried us more was the "One State" conference – organized by the Palestinians on campus during the time the BDS was still a fringe, toothless movement (that is, until Benjamin Netanyahu marked it as an enemy and significantly increased its profile and thus, status). Many in HKS hosted similar conventions concerning their own countries – for example, India and Brazil – and I wondered how an Israeli one hadn't happened yet.

On one of my morning runs along the Charles, I came across Zaki Djemal, an Israeli Harvard undergrad student, who was cycling by the river. Our talk on that sunny Boston day led to the decision to form our own Israeli conference. After reaching out to Israelis at Harvard, a few of us arranged a meetup – every Sunday at 11 in the morning. We'd join for coffee, work on our plan, and map out the things we wanted to speak about. We all agreed that we needed to go beyond the Israeli-Palestinian conflict and that we needed to recruit the first strong guest speaker, who would then attract others. Klarman and Jacobson donated $100,000 this time, and the Schusterman Foundation, who fully believed in me, added another $25,000. I won't forget the day I told my friends, via an email: "We have the *Nagid* (governor)!" – Stanley Fischer agreed to fly to our conference at HKS. After getting him on board, it was easier to recruit others, like hi-tech entrepreneur Dov Moran (Inventor of the USB memory stick); Dennis Ross, the Jewish American diplomat who served as Bill Clinton's special envoy to the Middle East; Dan Senor, co-author of the best-seller "Start-Up Nation" and Yariv Bash, who had just founded SpaceIL at the time, which later launched the first Israeli spacecraft. We took care of the preliminary public relations and made sure to hype up the event. At the time, newspapers ran articles about our conference, headlined: "Hitting Back at Harvard" in reference to the One State conference that was in the making.

All of the tickets to the Israel Conference were sold, and more than 900 people attended. In the preliminary cocktail mingling, Alan Dershowitz, the famous Jewish jurist and author, was also present. I kicked off the opening night, hosted by Becky Griffin (Israeli TV presenter) in the prestigious hall of the business school, with an emotional speech about this historic event, organized by Israeli students and led by their passion to present their country to the world. The event was preceded by a competition of plan proposals for promoting peace in the Middle East. On the second day of the conference, the winner was announced, who proposed a program that excited Dennis Ross as well and was awarded a humble gift of $1,000. Israel was presented as a country promoting innovation across many fields, and as a source of social entrepreneurship.

The decision to invest so much time, during a stressful study period, to host large outreach events, was certainly not trivial, but I don't regret it one bit. I couldn't accept the fact that intellectuals with so much influence, whom I shared a classroom with, were walking around with such a skewed perception of Israel. During that specific point in time, with all the strength and skills I had as a person thinking outside the box, I had the power to change it, to spark a butterfly effect in Harvard and beyond.

I never imagined at the time that I'd also gain personal benefit from these actions, that I'd get attractive job offers and have potential employers fight over me. But that's what happens when you follow your passion – marvelous surprises and fascinating opportunities come your way.

***

At the end of the first school year in HKS, everyone's mind races with the same burning question: Where will they intern during their summer break? Internships, whether in the public or private sphere, aren't mandatory, but the general thought is that a successful internship will help you find a good job after graduation. The somewhat obsessive preoccupation with internships – students prepare portfolios and go through interviews in a kind of internship fair at HKS – detracts, in my opinion, from the joy of school and the experience of being a student. While it's important to find the right internship, you shouldn't go overboard.

As a foreign student, it was harder for me to find a place to intern because I lacked American citizenship, and not all doors were open for me. I asked myself what I'd do in the summer. Mere idleness is out of the question at Harvard.

The opportunity came along from a different direction. The entrepreneurship bug that bit me while helping create "Comtribute" kept growing in size and led me to the next start-up I formed in the second semester of my first year, along with Gil Mendelson, an Israeli friend who worked with me at Comtribute. The objective of the company, which we called CareerVibes, was to create a website where people searched for the career best suited for them, a website where they could hear interviews by people from different fields talk about their journeys and career paths, as a way to learn from the unique perspective they offered. It was the start of the era of online videos, and the assumption was that you could learn about different professions across the globe and reach out through distinct media outlets, more accessible and tailor-suited for the user.

We presented our start-up at HKS's entrepreneurship forum and managed to raise $100,000, enough to get us going. We bought a camera and a tripod and I spent days interviewing and recording my classmates at Harvard. I used the connections I had made along the way – students who participated in the Israeli trek, for example – to reach out to interesting individuals who spoke about their work and shared valuable tips and insights they had accumulated. Thanks to this start-up, we were accepted into an exclusive program offered by General Electric and OMD, one of the largest media agencies in the world. As part of the program, I was invited to New York in the summer to participate in their start-up accelerator program, a format bringing together ten students proposing different ventures to change the world. We received all of the tools needed for success and were exempt from sharing its profits, which is what most accelerators demand.

Hence, I spent a wonderful summer in New York, one of the world's leading start-up cities. The program funded everything – the renovated apartment I rented with 2 HKS classmates on the sixth floor of a building, with no elevator, on the Lower East Side, the oldest neighborhood in south-east Manhattan, as well as a $4,000 scholarship bonus. In the mornings, we enjoyed what the program had to offer, like meetings with public opinion leaders and a supporting framework for building our ventures in OMD's insane offices. During our free time, we enjoyed all that Manhattan had to offer: bars and rooftop parties, baseball games, and jogging around Central Park.

At summer's end, I presented our idea to a panel of judges, and the winners were promised a nice sum of money and recognition. We competed against talented entrepreneurs, some of whom turned their ideas into successful companies. The night before the competition, I barely managed a wink of sleep. We worked hard on our presentation, right to the last minute, and the result was that I was a bit off by the time we presented it. I wrote a note to my future self that day: it's better to sleep another two hours at night. We didn't win, nor did the company materialize to officially launch, but I certainly enjoyed every minute spent in New York.

***

Life continued to flow beautifully in the Republic of Cambridge, as this group of experienced and talented young people put their lives on hold for two years, devoting themselves to the full experience of being students. We were 28, serious and composed, but also drunk on everything Harvard had to offer. We danced at Harvard's balls, played beer pong at house parties, and watched the film "The Social Network" (that had just come out that year) at the Harvard Square cinema – the place where those very events unfolded. In the summer, we went on vacations to Puerto Rico, and in the winter, ski trips to Vermont.

On autumn break during the second year, Josh and I flew to New Orleans to visit his sister Naomi. Together with her and a group of her college friends, we partied at Mardi Gras, the city's world-renowned festival. We flew back on Continental Airlines, and our flight was delayed numerous times. But just when Josh needed to go to the bathroom, boarding began. Seconds before he returned, the gate closed on us and didn't open no matter how much we begged. While we tried to get the most out of life and party as hard as we could, we were still two, relatively poor Harvard students. So we went for the cheap option: we bought a ticket to New York with Jet Blue Airlines, and in Chinatown, boarded a night bus to take us to Boston. Like two typical nerds, we wrote a letter to Continental Airlines' CEO – a Harvard alum who we believed would be compassionate enough to help us – demanding our money back, but the letter didn't impress him much. My skills in obtaining compensation from airline companies would improve later in life.

This was a very different experience from the "rat race" students spiral into in Israel, from juggling school and a mundane job just to fund a tiny, shared apartment. The experience at Harvard was far more uniting. The American theme promotes unity, but at the same time, rivalry. From our apartment on the 21st floor, we watched the regatta, a series of boat races across the Charles River. However, the pinnacle of university rivalry is, of course, the annual Harvard vs. Yale football game. Even though both teams are pretty bad, it's about ethos – on the wall of Harvard's bar hangs the results of the games over the years – and it's an experience no Harvard student who respects themselves would dare to miss. Together, we took a bus to New Haven and showed up drunk at the field, keeping with the American tradition.

The second year at Harvard was even better due to my love story with Pamela, a talented girl who enrolled with me in HKS while doing a joint degree with Harvard Business School (the best study option in my opinion, combining public policy and business in three years). Pam, an American from Virginia, the daughter of an

American mother and Indian father, was one of the reasons I wanted to stay in America. The fact that she wasn't Jewish sprung to mind occasionally, but at that point, it mostly worried my bubby.

Another source of pride during my second year was helping people get into Harvard through working at a company that helps prospective students prepare their applications, and I accompanied an applicant throughout her admissions process. Eventually, she was accepted, and in light of the fact that she was my only protege, I gave myself a 100% success rate.

***

In line with HKS's practical approach, grad students don't hand in a research thesis when they graduate, but rather, a PAE (Policy Analysis Exercise) – a consulting project, the highlight of their second year. As part of the project, students need to find themselves a client and help them solve an issue they are grappling with. The fact that we were Harvard graduates made it easier to get clients.

Due to my experience with Comtribute, I knew I wanted my project to focus on Social Impact. The field of Corporate Social Responsibility, a contribution to society according to the ethos of the organization in a way that would provide value for the community, was then, back in 2011, a hot global trend, but practically nonexistent in Israel. Thanks to my connections with Seth Cohen, the Schusterman Foundation's Network Director, I offered to conduct my project on Social Impact in Israel under the foundation's umbrella. I knew it was the right link for me. I assumed that not only would it grant me the flexibility and resources necessary for the project, if I offered the foundation a valuable plan, as I intended to do, there was a chance it would also be implemented. I had already started thinking about my path onward and fully believed that this project would reveal my skills, potentially leading to a job offer upon graduation. Seth, from his end, had no reason to turn down my offer of a free consulting project from a Harvard student.

Students choose mentors to guide them throughout the project, and the wide array of professors – people who have achieved quite a lot in their lives, both in and outside of academia – makes the experience even better. Among these experienced people was, for example, David Gergen, senior political analyst for CNN and the manager of several presidential campaigns. I chose Richard (Dick) Cavanagh, one of the social corporate responsibility pioneers, and the founder of this business model at McKinsey & Company. I used the annual grant that was at my disposal as a member of the ROI community and flew to meetings with people in Israel. I was supported by foundations and organizations involved in the field, such as "Yad Hanadiv" (my friend Elad Katz, who worked at the foundation, shared his insights with me) and Ashoka, an international organization uniting leading social entrepreneurs of the world.

My thesis, which was one of the first ones written in Israel on the topic, suggested introducing the field with the help of an accelerator (akin to the one in New York), by then a very common approach in America and less developed in Israel. The idea was to build an accelerator that united business entrepreneurs and social entrepreneurs to create a fruitful synergy. This time around, I veered from my "B" average and got an "A-" on the project.

***

My parents and bubby flew in for my emotional graduation, to see with their own eyes that their offspring was indeed a Harvard graduate. It made me happy to have them there, and I know they were happy as well. By the time I finished school, I already knew I wanted to continue living in the U.S., at least for the time being. Looking for a job while graduates around me were landing positions one by one was stressful, to say the least. In my case, though, the pressure was twofold: If I didn't find a job, I knew I wouldn't be able to get a visa and would have to part ways with Pam. I received many rejections from several companies in a wide array of fields, and some didn't even reply to my initial application.

The decision to do my thesis for the Schusterman Foundation proved to be the right one, as I was offered the job to be their Program Officer in Atlanta. I received a similar offer from a philanthropic foundation in Boston that I respected tremendously. The fact that I had two job offers allowed me to play them against each other and ask for better terms. I knew that the Schusterman Foundation wouldn't want to lose me to another Jewish foundation. An ego thing.

I also knew, despite the deliberation, that Schusterman was the better choice for me at that point. Its spirit, by the nature of the work, promoted a balance of work and pleasure in a young environment and better suited my needs than the heavier, more financial orientation of the second foundation, which, although different, was no less amazing. I already knew Seth Cohen, and knew we worked great together. I assumed the Schusterman Foundation would grant me a sense of that freedom I desperately needed. It was, in fact, my first workplace in the U.S., and I wanted to fit in easily. Excel sheets weren't my forte, and I felt that at this point, I needed to work on my strengths, not my weaknesses. The right time would come to take care of them as well.

I'm a true believer in gut feelings, and that the right thing to do isn't just chase a higher paycheck or prestige, rather, examine where you can best develop yourself while still feeling comfortable enough to maximize your skills. Despite the difficulty of leaving Boston for the much less tempting Atlanta, and having to distance myself from Pam, who had another year of school before her, I set out on a new path.

I continued on my journey to my third station in North America. This time, I was headed south.

My Word to the Wise

- When choosing between two options, follow your gut feeling. Make sure you don't agree to an offer only because it pays more, but rather, see if it's the right choice for you, the right place where you can be your best self.
- Maximize any opportunity or chance that comes your way. Be open to the possible changes that may land you in a different place than the one you had planned.
- Scout for mentors, inspiring people who have reached certain milestones in life and can advise you on your path forward.
- Ask yourself at any given time and decision point, what you are looking to optimize for. The answer at different points in time will be different, but that's what should guide your decision tree.

A Word to the Wise by
TOMER COHEN, CEO of BUYME

Key to Success:
A Solid Plan and a Winning Brain Trust

There's no such thing as a task too big, no such thing as a job that's "out of your league." If you plan things out meticulously, to the smallest of details, and form your own brain trust of good people who have your interests in mind, there's nothing in the world you won't be able to accomplish.

What is this brain trust? A group of people with whom you can have unfiltered conversations, guided by one solid interest: to ensure your success. This can be a family member, a good friend, or a guiding mentor. The principles stay the same: they care for your success, they provide a candid reflection of yourself so you can learn and grow, and there's a motivating attitude driving you forward toward your goals.

After serving in the army for nearly five years (four of them as an officer in the Paratroopers Brigade and one in the IDF Spokesperson's Unit), I joined the political sector in media-related and spokesman positions. I worked for the center-left Yesh Atid party, and when it joined the ruling coalition, I decided I wanted to move on to a position that, at the time, seemed out of reach: chief of staff. In other words, the person charged with implementing the minister's policies internally and externally, opposite other government ministries. He's the chief advisor, the primary buffer between the minister and everyone else, and the one who manages the entire 12-person administrative staff.

At the age of 23, with no degree or experience in management, I put myself out there and offered to be the chief of staff of Yaakov Peri, Israel's former Minister of Innovation, Science, and Technology. I met with five former chiefs of staff, and with the help of my loyal brain trust, devised a written plan, spread across a large number of pages, and rehearsed my pitch to Peri. I acted as if I had already landed the job. In our first conversation, I presented a detailed work plan outlining the future steps I'd take to succeed in the job and laid out several arguments explaining why I was fit for this role. My pitch ended with: "The plan is already written and set. If you decide not to hire me, I'll gladly pass it on to whoever you do so they can ensure you succeed."

In the end, I got the job and spent the next couple of months coping with a sense of immense pressure weighing down on me. I was scared someone would "expose" me, expose the fact that I didn't actually know what I was doing. But I managed to do it, thanks to my detailed plan and the close group of people who guided me, serving as a lighthouse in the many storms to come.

Peri, who was head of the "Shin Bet" (Israel's domestic clandestine security agency) as well as CEO of a major cellphone company and chairman of a central bank, had worked with many managers in his life before meeting me. But he had faith in my work, and his confidence accompanies me to this day. He chose me as head of his team, the person closest to him, even though I had no experience in management or government work. But I came ready with a plan, an extremely detailed one. A few years later, I asked Peri why he decided to hire me, and he replied: "I believed in you. I saw that whatever knowledge you lacked, you would learn and make up for it fast. And that is what makes a good manager."

Since then, I have carefully planned out every aspect of my professional life. Any position, any goal, as well as every failure and disappointment, is always scrutinized under the lens of "planning versus execution." Peri gave me valuable insight: with proper planning and a supportive environment, anything is possible.

CHAPTER 6

Atlanta

From Downfalls to New Heights

The transition from the grand, lofty heights of Harvard to a new job in a foreign city, in a new state, was difficult…far more so than I expected.

It was my fourth big transition in three years: from Jerusalem to Montreal, to Cambridge, and now Atlanta, Georgia's capital and America's "Capital of the South." I was continuing my exploration of North America – shifting from its eastern seaboard southward – from the freezing cold of Boston to "Hotlanta." Being as I'm a pretty minimalistic person, I rolled into my new apartment with two humble suitcases from which I began unpacking my new life, or at least I tried to.

From the jump, during my very first chat with the security guard of the complex in which I decided to rent an apartment, I realized I'd arrived to a completely different America, with aspects and characteristics foreign to me. The giant complex was right in midtown Atlanta, in front of the "W Hotel" and Piedmont Park. It had a lobby, a cinema room, a pool, and a gym. America at its finest. My spiffy apartment, number 409, overlooked the pool, and it cost the same as the room I'd rented and shared in the Soviet-style Harvard dorm. On my first day, I wanted to buy milk for my morning coffee, so I asked the guard where the closest minimarket was. "10th Street," he said and pointed in the direction. "Right around the corner, a five-minute walk, but I'm not sure you'll find parking." In other words: Welcome to America's lazy South, where people don't walk, not even if they live right in the center of the city. The culture was different, the ambiance was foreign, the cost of living was far cheaper; even the food was different – good old comfort food. If you wanted fried green tomatoes or mac & cheese, you were in the right place. I am, after all, a person who likes experiencing new things, and here I was, in this amusement park full of new opportunities. But even the most exciting amusement parks require a certain amount of getting used to before racing to explore the new rides.

I quickly organized my apartment – furnishing it with a bed, couch, TV, and cereal – and settled into my new workplace in one of the offices rented by Schusterman in Atlanta's Jewish Federation building.

During my first days at work, I felt distracted and disoriented. Sitting in a cramped room in the federation's building, I often wondered what I was doing there and whether I'd made the right decision. After three years of being surrounded by friends and stimuli, I felt quite lonely, far from Pam, the girlfriend I left behind. This new job, the one I chose, seemed dull and uninspiring.

I would later learn that this "Post-Harvard" syndrome

is quite common among graduates of the university, as well as graduates in general who step out into the "real world." Conan O'Brien, a Harvard alum himself, dedicated a full comedy sketch to it called "The Harvard Syndrome": the downfall from the summit of Harvard – a prestigious place where I was surrounded by intelligent people and was able to combine a love of knowledge with just as much fun – to the real world involving a stringent routine that isn't easy getting used to. In fact, one study has shown that most Harvard graduates aren't satisfied with their workplace during their first few years out of the university. I think academic institutions invest so much in their students during school that they forget how important it is to guide them on their way out as well. I have a dream (as a former resident of the city in which he was born and buried, allow me to quote Martin Luther King) to speak in front of Harvard's graduate committee, present them with this phenomenon, and convince them to use the tools they already have to help alums on their way out – an investment that will surely reap benefits. In my opinion, if they did this, the performance of graduates would skyrocket, and more importantly, their affiliation with Harvard would also be reflected in their potential contribution to it later on.

In retrospect, I can say that I was slightly depressed at that time. Barely managing to function, I continuously dwelled over my situation in life. It was a low point I was scared I wouldn't recover from. My kind and wise mother, who picked up on my sadness over the phone, bought my sister, Leety, a flight ticket to Atlanta right after we hung up. Leety, a graduate of industrial design and a woman who is no less amazing than my mom, passed on her final school project, helped me unpack my bags, and turned my new apartment into a home. She went on hikes with me around the area and helped me snap back to my physical exercise routine.

Slowly but surely, my energy was replenished. Through this experience, I learned how to pick myself up before I collapsed. Every person needs to find what helps them in times of need, and for me, exercising is a huge savior. Nowadays, one down moment is enough to get me out and running.

Pam struggled to cope with my mood swings, and we ended up splitting up. Relationships, as noted by wise folks before me, are tested in times of struggle. In those difficult moments, I discovered the loyalty of my family. And in line with the usual theme of my romantic life, Pam ended up marrying the first guy she met after we broke up – a good friend of hers from before – Josh Harder, now a congressman, who was also on the Israel trek.

***

When I was no longer struggling to acclimatize, my new job really opened up. In came a rush of fascinating challenges, ones I truly enjoyed working through.

Seth and I had a goal to locate influential, young Jews, under the age of 40, who weren't connected with Israel, nor Judaism in general, and bring them closer to the Jewish world and Israel, mapping out new opportunities to create that connection. Up until then, the Schusterman Foundation mostly focused on Jews who were already involved in the community anyhow, and never really reached out to those who weren't infatuated with Israel, or who weren't an integrative part of the Jewish community.

Seth and I had plenty of freedom to explore this immense potential, which could easily be squandered, as there isn't one fixed way to plug these young people into the community. While we seemingly started from scratch, I did have numerous tools at my disposal: my entrepreneurial experience, the network of people I'd accumulated, which was by then large and diverse, and the many stations I'd visited along the way – summer camp in Malibu, working at Hillel at the Hebrew University, and advocating for the Israel I know in Canada and Harvard.

The Schusterman Foundation was looking to overcome a challenge I'd already encountered from different angles: discovering the right hook to reel in young Jews so they can connect to Judaism and Israel in a way suitable for them.

Moreover, I had an inherent advantage at my disposal. I, myself, was an example of someone who chose to stay in the country out of his own free will. I was born to foreign parents, immigrants who took a brave step and chose to live in Israel at a point in time when the reasons for forging a connection with the land and people were different: pioneering, kibbutz life, idealism, old-school Zionism. What worked for me could work for others. And I had another advantage, which is part of my personality: I'm a people person, one who can find a common language with nearly anyone. It's easy for me to generate empathy, which I believe is the core of any sales endeavor, whether its Dead Sea products or Judaism and Israel. I utilize my strengths and advantages to get ahead, sharpen my skills and learn more.

It's far easier to succeed in a job you believe in and vibe with, and I, personally, derived great pleasure from mine. I got to explore places I enjoyed. Right off the bat, Seth and I realized that every potential person, whether they came from hi-tech, art, or gaming, required a distinct work plan, so the two of us embarked on a fascinating journey to research the different fields. We interviewed people from San Francisco, Austin, and New York, and brainstormed with young Jews from Boston. We took part in fun experiences, full of the types of people we were targeting, like the South By Southwest (SXSW) Festival in Austin – a cultural celebration involving cinema, music, hi-tech, standup comedy, and even political panels.

At that time, in 2012, hackathons were tremendously popular, and we concluded that they were a fantastic and authentic platform for connecting Israel and Jews living in America. With the help of the "Public Knowledge Workshop," an association working to make data in Israel more accessible to its citizens, we launched a hackathon between San Francisco and Israel. For 36 hours straight, people from both ends worked to find solutions for challenging issues concerning the Jewish world (issues the Schusterman Foundation was trying to solve). The result: an app built for BBYO, temporarily called "Schmooze," whose goal was to help Jewish students find roommates in over 10,000 universities from coast to coast in the U.S. "In the past, Zionism meant draining the malaria-ridden swamps; today, it's an iPhone app, and, for at least one weekend in San Francisco, it was just as riveting," a news reporter from one of Israel's main papers wrote as she accompanied our hackathon.

It was a major success, except for one little thing: we called our hackathon "Friday Night Hack" – not the best name for an event centered around a religion for which the Sabbath, which begins Friday evening, is a holy day of rest. Lynn Schusterman loved the concept but was much less thrilled with the criticism we got for being a Jewish foundation that runs hackathons on the Sabbath. Moral of the story: even when you try shaking things up, it's better to shake gently, especially when you're working for a major philanthropic figure who runs the show.

We paved our path into the gaming world with the help of Asi Burak, an Israeli who lives in New York and founded "Games for Change," an organization developing games advocating social change. Together, we created a gaming competition relating to the Jewish world, with a prize of $25,000 for whoever created the winning prototype for a computer game. We asked a few organizations to provide us with some challenges and chose the one presented by SpaceIL – an educational game about Israel's first spacecraft. I worked on the project with Kfir Damari, SpaceIL's founder. The winning game was chosen for a festival hosted in Tribeca, New York, and was widely praised.

In the belief that leading organizations in the Jewish world have the potential to unite people through different alumni associations, we established a million-dollar fund to promote the issue. The grants were awarded to leading organizations with whom we worked to foster continuity. Among them were "StandWithUs Israel" and "The Sky Isn't the Limit," (an organization of Israeli Air Force veterans).

As part of our research, Seth became immersed in a community founded by four people who, after graduating from prestigious universities, found themselves jobless due to the 2008 financial crisis. They decided to create their own alternative and formed the Summit Series, which would later become a leading community that creates vibrant user experiences, connecting art, music, hi-tech, real estate, and more. The founders purchased Powder Mountain in Eden, Utah for $40 million, a resort that includes ski trails and a lake, and which now serves as a place for the community's gatherings. The biggest one is their annual summit, considered the Davos Forum of Generation Y. It lasts for several days and attracts successful people from all over the world. Among its speakers have been Bill Clinton, Napster founder Sean Parker, and mega-mogul Richard Branson.

Members of the community include the founders of Facebook and MySpace, Warren Buffet's grandson, the granddaughter of former President George Bush as well as two Israeli women: actress and producer Noa Tishby, and entrepreneur Galia Benartzi founder of Bancor, a blockchain company. This community was just the right place for us: many of those who join are Jews. Following in Seth's footsteps, I also traveled to the city of Eden, and in search of the right tie between the place and our foundation's goal, the crowning glory of our mission was born: The newly formed Reality Trip – a journey to Israel for young influencers from around the world.

"From Eden to Zion" was the first journey to launch and provided the driving force.

The idea was to take fifty members of the Summit Series community (the number of people who could fit in a bus) and take them on an exceptional journey around Israel.

While it was predicated on other existing trips (like the Harvard treks, "Taglit" trips, and ITreks) we wanted to frame and orchestrate it differently. Schusterman had already established successful Reality trips for Teach For America members and leading educators with an itinerary geared toward leadership, with Israel serving as a prism through which to experience growth and transformation. We wanted to expand upon that while targeting a vastly different population from the aforementioned trips. With the connections to Noa and Galia, we were able to pick out with precision a group of unique individuals. We faced a difficult challenge: the foundation was suspected by some of promoting what was perceived as a form of missionary work. We were walking a tightrope. I thoroughly enjoyed building the itinerary and recruiting people. Most of the funding – about $6,000 a person – came from the foundation, whereas the participants paid a symbolic fee of $750. We managed to recruit actress Sophia Bush, Slava Rubin (the founder of Indiegogo) and many more.

In April 2016, our first Reality excursion landed in Israel. Before the journey, I told the participants: "If you leave Israel with fewer questions than you came with, this means we did something wrong." But we succeeded, big time: a week later, the participants left the country with a host of questions, yet with happy, satisfied, and enlightened expressions on their faces following what they learned. We earned fifty great ambassadors who paved the way for more to come.

***

To understand the impact of the trip and the stirring effect it had on the participants, I have to elaborate on each of the carefully chosen stations along the journey.

The trip began in a park called "Neot Kdumim," located in the Ben Shemen Forest, a landscape that offers a glimpse into the land of the Bible. Against the backdrop of gunfire sounds from the nearby military base, the fifty overwhelmed participants were immediately thrust out of their comfort zone and sent to herd a flock of sheep. Thus, the first leadership insight was duly noted: to lead, you must station yourself in the rear, rather than the front, and from that point, lead onwards. An additional conclusion surfaced – pay careful attention to our instructions: even though we told them to bring comfortable shoes, many of them came with flip-flops or even high heels and wallowed over the bitter mistake they had made.

The second day in Tel Aviv – a city like no other – was dedicated to connecting the theme of the group with Israel: a start-up nation, a community striving to create a better world. We visited the "SOSA" start-up complex in the south of the city, where we met with several entrepreneurs, among them Shai Agassi, who talked about the failure of his company "Better Place." One can learn as much from failures as from success stories, possibly even more. In the evening, we held a networking event with Israeli public opinion leaders, some of whom had been a part of the Summit Series community, like the singer Ivri Lider, with whom we jammed one night.

The following morning began like every morning on the trip, with a gratitude ceremony delivered by a different participant. We then left Tel Aviv and traveled to Mikhmoret Beach. With the sound of the waves swaying in the background, we spoke about the four types of leaders who led the Jews out of Egypt, a method that I first learned from Avraham Infeld, President Emeritus of Hillel.

A leader's role is to move people from place to place, physically, emotionally, and ideologically, just like the shepherd, who must move his herd around or else fail in his vocation.

The interesting thing about the Exodus story is that G-d didn't create one leader who could have theoretically freed the Jews from Egypt's hold easily, rather, he formed a four-member board of directors.

The first was Moses, the CEO, and let's be real: I doubt anyone would hire him today. From the details written in the Bible, Moses lacked all of the qualities we now attribute to leaders: he stuttered, wasn't very popular (many complained about him and wondered where he was taking them), he shoved his nose into other people's business (particularly arguments), he spoke non-stop and rarely stopped to listen. He wasn't even good at administrative work: Moses never heard of proper delegation. Despite all of these limitations and disadvantages, he became the greatest leader in history for one reason only: he was driven by a deep calling and a clear vision. He knew exactly where he wanted to lead his people. Nothing diverted him from the task at hand, not the desire to be popular nor the temptations offered.

But Moses wasn't alone, and in came his brother Aaron, who couldn't be more different: the classic Chief Communications Officer. A pursuer of peace, beloved by all, attentive, coherent, articulate, and capable of finding common ground with nearly everyone – he spoke with Pharaoh in one way, and with the Israelites in another. A preacher who knew how to take complex ideas and unpack them in simple language. The Israelites, who didn't shed a tear when Moses died, cried 30 days straight after Aaron passed.

Both brothers knew how to work together, but when Moses was called by the chairman of the executive committee for a board meeting at the top of the mountain, spread across 40 days and 40 nights, he entrusted the nation to Aaron, and a serious blunder occurred: the Israelites built the golden calf. That's precisely what happens when you lead without a vision in mind – your followers will build a golden calf behind your back.

Even the duo of Moses and Aaron alone couldn't bring the Israelites into the Holy Land because they put too much emphasis on the mind, and not enough on the heart. To move people, one should turn to their hearts. Thus, Moses and Aaron's team was joined by their sister, Miriam, who, according to the Bible, didn't really speak too much. She dances, sings, and plays the drums – representing the spirit and soul of the Israelites, the one who leads the people through her passion. She would be classified as Chief People Officer in today's world. Each team needs a passionate leader. In times of ease, complex ideas can be delivered quite simply, but challenging moments like crossing the Red Sea with kids and baggage calls for a person who can provide some creative value to the mission, and foster a trend of growth among the community, bolstering its members' loyalty even in dire times.

This team of three was enough to get the Jews out of Egypt and across the desert, but not enough to bring them into the Holy Land. Why?

Because none of them knew how to open a computer or manage an Excel sheet. Everything they comprised – Moses' vision, Aaron's altruism, and Miriam's passion – had to be transformed into an actual, practical plan, and luckily, G-d brought in Joshua, the team's Chief Operating Officer. He was the one who divided the nation into tribes and gave each one a task and instructions on delivering it. Every organization knows there is a decisive moment in which it must translate the messages into numbers and arrange them on an Excel sheet for all members to understand and proceed from, which tasks to do, and which responsibilities to undertake. Welcome Joshua, we've been waiting for you. From this point on, it wasn't just a walk across the desert, rather, there was a daily routine to sustain. At the end of the day, Joshua was the leader who completed the task and brought the Israelites to their coveted destination.

Throughout the "Reality" journey in Israel, each one of the participants also went through their own personal journey to the core of their leadership values. We used the Exodus as a framework through which to discuss the topic in small groups, as well as in a large forum. The diverse team G-d had created, a team with four distinct types of leaders, succeeded in getting the Jews out of Egypt, across the desert, and into Israel. A task of this order wasn't meant for one leader, or one CEO, but rather, a whole team. When a leader recruits other members, they first need to know themselves, their weaknesses and strengths, so they can find the right people to complement what they lack. And before embarking on the journey, they will need to determine their mission and vision, for it is impossible to lead without them.

We wrapped up our trip to Mikhmoret Beach with a raft-building competition, and on our way to the north of the country, we stopped at a kibbutz called Ma'agan Michael, to hear about socialist kibbutz values. We met with the CEO of Plasson (a successful plastic pipe company), an older, jovial member of the kibbutz who presided over a successful factory. We witnessed the oxymoron up close: kibbutzim that weren't privatized made a lot of money. I spoke about my experience as someone who grew up on a kibbutz, and we discussed billion-dollar ideas that were hatched on kibbutzim. For example Adam Neumann, the founder of WeWork, always said that he got the idea of a shared working space from his upbringing on Kibbutz Nir Am. Another enterprise, Zipcar, is a car-sharing service established on those same values.[4]

Finally, we reached my childhood home – the Golan

---

[4]. In fact, the kibbutz actually came up with this idea many years ago, but since they were not businessmen, they didn't know how to monetize it.

Heights. We left Kibbutz Merom Golan on ATVs for a structure that once served as a Syrian army headquarters, not far from the border. Amid the backdrop of gunfire and explosions from the civil war raging right across the border, our tour guide, Michael Bauer (an exceptional guide and storyteller) provided us with stories on the geopolitical climate. All the participants were baffled. Throughout the journey, stark contrasts stood out (discrepancies that we Israelis are used to), like the sharp transition from a fun ATV ride along colorful graffiti paintings done by Israel's finest artists to the clear and present sounds of war nearby – akin to the quick transition from the mournful songs and ceremonies on Israel's Memorial Day, and the festivities and fireworks a few hours later when the country welcomes its Independence Day. Only after seeing the expressions of foreigners coming from New York and LA, places in which bombings are an anomaly, does one understand how, what appears to Israelis as trivial, is so utterly abnormal.

The echoes of war accompanied us to my beloved Mt. Bental. They also made it easier to understand why Israel must never give up a strategic plateau such as the Golan Heights, and certainly not amid a raging civil war.

An important part of forming this journey was figuring out what interested each group. In this case, given the emphasis on community building, it was obvious that we needed to take them up the mountain at sunset. It was the right decision.

We finished that emotional day at a local winery near Kidmat Tzvi, an agricultural community, or "*moshav*." The expansive landscape of the vineyard gave us room to process all that we'd experienced, and the character of the place itself coincided with the character of the group. The winery was founded by a family whose son went to school with me, and with whom I played basketball. We were told about the formation of the winery over a splendid dinner accompanied by their finest wines. As the sky grew dark, we lit a cozy bonfire, a perfect ending to this long, enriching day.

On the fifth day, we ventured to the Dead Sea and the Jordan Rift Valley for an equally emotional time. After members of the trip saw the Syrian and Lebanese border on the previous day, this time, they got to take a close look at the Jordanian border. Through the tunnel leading to Mount Scopus, as Matisyahu's song "Jerusalem (Out of Darkness Comes Light)" played on the bus, the ancient city was revealed before our eyes, in all its glory. Ensuring that the travel experience was on point was no less important: the arrival in Jerusalem at the climax of the journey when the complexities of the country had already been laid out bore its fruit. The participants were euphoric and began dancing on the bus.

We gave them enough time to explore the city, soak up the experience and take pictures. We discussed the Schusterman family, the people behind this journey who also donate a significant portion of their wealth to Jerusalem, and wandered across the alleys of the Old City – the Armenian Quarter, the Muslim Quarter, the Church of the Holy Sepulchre, all the way to the Western Wall. We stayed at the Mamilla Hotel, just outside the Old City's walls, where we met with young leaders from an organization called MEET (Middle East Entrepreneurs of Tomorrow), which focuses on creating an active network of young Palestinians and Israelis through a common interest in technology, entrepreneurship, and problem-solving. The participants easily connected with these young leaders through their stories, and after getting to know them, many even decided to donate to the organization. On another trip, composed of people in the hi-tech sector, one of the participants confessed how moved they felt after meeting the kids, and asked the group to donate to MEET. They managed to raise $25,000, and the Schusterman Foundation added, via a matching system, a similar sum. This was a perfect example of one of the trip's objectives we had discussed on Mikhmoret Beach – moving from the passive to the active, an actual call for action.

As evening cast over Jerusalem, we walked through the Nahlaot neighborhood, one of the most special neighborhoods in the world, with its narrow alleyways and picturesque buildings made of Jerusalem stone. The Rivlin family, of which I am a descendant, was one of the seven families that ventured outside the Old City's walls and founded the neighborhood. We reached the house of the late artist Yoram Amir, an extraordinary man, an exceptional storyteller, and a Jerusalemite at heart. From his house, we wandered off to the Mahane Yehuda market, a place bustling with vegetable and fruit stands during the day, and a spot brimming with bars and restaurants at night, where Jews and Arabs, secular and religious, the young and old, and locals and tourists can meet.

Along with her husband Lior Shabo, Karen Brunwasser, co-director of "The Jerusalem Season of Culture," which is supported by the Schusterman Foundation, created an introductory brochure of the market, sending our participants on a special and informative tour along its colorful alleys, where they enjoyed beer tastings and *jahnun*, a Yemenite Jewish pastry. As the clock struck midnight, we ended the day at Machneyuda restaurant with a joyous celebration of desserts and dancing as a way to connect the micro and the macro. As their feet danced wildly on the restaurant tables, there was a sense of integration – the personal journey with the communal experience.

On Friday, after a necessary and emotional visit to the Yad Vashem Holocaust museum, we began preparing ourselves for the Sabbath, a transition between the mundane and holy. Wearing all white, we met on the hotel roof. Keeping with the idea that members of the group were active participants on this journey – it is only through active self-expression that we connect – one of them hosted the *kabalat Shabbat* ("welcoming the Sabbath") ceremony in light of this special moment.

We gathered back in the Old City for a nighttime view of the Western Wall, which, on this day of the week, is crammed with people praying – vastly different from the daytime experience. Our special dinner was held at the "Harp of David," the unique house of the artist Arik Pelzig. The house contains rooms dug underground, halls with curved ceilings and a bunker that served as a forward operating position during Israel's War of Independence. It overlooks the Old City and is located ten yards from the place where the Last Supper was held. Meeting the landlord, a remarkable man, made the experience even more impactful. Enveloped with a sense of community, the trip's members shared what Sabbath means to them – whether they had celebrated it in the past or were finding out about it just now. This was an incredibly special point in the journey, where the emphasis wasn't placed solely on religion, but rather on Jewish rituals that hold value for people worldwide – a day of rest, self-care, and connection with loved ones, a magical transition between the mundane and the holy, and vice versa.

On Saturday morning, we bid farewell to Jerusalem. And with this sense of spiritual ascension, we continued to Masada – a popular tourist site that allows for another glimpse at a challenging leadership dilemma – and to the lowest place on Earth, the Dead Sea. After some fun in the mud, we went further south for the Sabbath "separation" ceremony, held at an equally unique place in Israel – the Great Crater. By this point, members of the trip were no longer a group, but rather, a close-knit family.

On our last night, the journey reached its apex at the beautiful Bereshit Hotel, a magical place overlooking vast plains of desert. The members didn't have much time to enjoy the luxurious facilities, because a little after arrival, we took them to a slightly different setting: solitude in the desert. Under a starlit sky, I told them about the seclusion ("*hitbodedut*") ritual, introduced by Rabbi Nachman of Breslov and the Hasidic Movement, which is all about connecting oneself to G-d, close to nature, where every blade of grass and small pebble prays with you, and sent them off to explore this ritual on their own. I asked them to wander in the desert and find a spot to seclude themselves, under the following conditions: for ten minutes, nonstop, they were to speak out loud – to themselves, to God, to the world. During these ten minutes, they could yell, say thanks, cry, preach, be angry, philosophize, protest this task and even curse the person who sent them off on this task, as long as they didn't stop talking until I'd instructed them otherwise.

When they returned, overwhelmed by the surge of emotions that washed over them during their seclusion, I finished with a story about a girl who preferred nature over sitting in the synagogue. One day, her grandpa followed her out of the synagogue and saw her praying in nature. When confronted with her actions, she explained: "I feel close to God when I'm in nature."

"Don't you know that G-d is the same everywhere?" wondered her grandpa.

"I know," she replied calmly, "but I'm not."

Down below, from the ravine, sounds of Bedouin music echoed. We walked along a candle-lit pathway that led to a large camp, where a warm dinner was waiting for us, ending with a bonfire and hookahs.

On our last day, right before the group would board the plane taking them home, two more stops awaited them. We gathered in Sde Boker, at the grave of David and Paula Ben-Gurion, where Michael, our tour guide, integrated everything we'd learned to unpack the story of Israel's formation. At the closing dinner in the Valley of Elah, at Hedai Offaim's special farm overlooking the Palestinian Authority's territories, Hedai shared his story, one of love, unity, food, and sustainable agriculture.

We held our closing at the farm and shared our thoughts on the life waiting for us back home, the way to savor the experience we'd been through and our connection to the Schusterman Foundation. I reminded this new "family" of what I'd said at the start of our journey: "If you return with fewer questions than those you came with, this means we did something wrong." We certainly didn't. Following this successful trip, twelve additional journeys were embarked upon every year, each one fine tuned to fit the group's overall character. On some trips, we put more emphasis on music and meditation. Even the hosts we met with changed according to the group. Among them, Jamila, a grandma who crafts handmade soap, and Margalit Zinati, "The Last Jew of Peki'in" – two astonishing women and inspiring pioneers, who provided another perspective from which to view leadership styles and Israel's complex narrative.

***

Back in Atlanta, I began feeling a real sense of connection with this new and interesting city I learned to love. A city where slavery flourished, but which produced Martin Luther King and served as the epicenter of America's civil rights movement; a city brimming with trade, industry, and economy, with the busiest airport in the U.S.; a city offering a wide range of cultural events, restaurants, and nightly hangouts; one with skyscrapers and trade centers, while simultaneously blooming with lush forests; a city in constant growth, but with Southern hospitality and a laidback lifestyle, much more relaxed compared to other big cities like New York and Chicago. What's not to love about such a place?

The pleasure I derived was even greater due to the many friends I made. Added to my circle of friends were people I met on "Reality" journeys, among them Justin Dangel, owner of a successful insurance company who took part in the first trip we launched. Dangel, a bright skeptic, a Democrat at heart who hadn't previously connected with Israel, was among those greatly affected by the visit. While in Israel, he was impressed by United Hatzalah, an emergency first aid NGO. He donated to the organization and formed a company called "Ready Responders," comprising a group of healthcare professionals who provide rapid medical services in cities across the U.S.

Dangel had two other lovely traditions: He would invite his friends over for Friday night dinners – a custom that many of the trip's participants picked up on their return home – and every year during Jazz Fest in New Orleans, he'd rent a house there and invite his friends to stay over.

Another friend I made on the trip was Okieriete "Oak" Onaodowan, who starred in the successful musical "Hamilton." After the Reality journey, Oak invited me and Seth to Broadway to see him perform and called us backstage (the fact that I fell asleep during the play says nothing about its quality and talented actors, it's just that I fall asleep practically everywhere).

At dinner at the home of Consul General Ofer Aviran, who greatly admired the foundation's activities, I met more interesting people, among them Tom Barry,

Israel's swimming team captain who'd become a close friend of mine. I loved visiting him at the University of Georgia where he studied and competed. He exposed me to all the glory college life had to offer. There, too, football games are a holy event. Unlike Harvard vs. Yale though, these guys actually know how to play. My friends from HKS came one after the other for visits, and I joined some Harvard students on a trek to Georgia. Along with my friends, I visited former President Jimmy Carter's peanut farm. He gave us a tour of the land and discussed fascinating stories with us. Something about the former president returning to nature reminded me of Israel's first prime minister, Ben-Gurion, returning to the kibbutz in the desert after his retirement.

Thanks to my friend Narkis Alon, I got to know India after she invited me to lecture at a conference focused on community building, hosted by one of India's largest philanthropists. While in India, I made a new friend who had also lectured there, Adi Altschuler, founder of the youth movement "Wings of Krembo," helping people with special needs. As a hoarder of new experiences, I took advantage of the invitation to Delhi and journeyed another five days to the north of the country.

I ventured all the way to Saint Petersburg in distant Russia to connect young Jews to the foundation's goals. While there, I also dealt with another critical mission. Seth Cohen and Sandy Cardin, CEO of the Schusterman Foundation, who were supposed to arrive along with Lynn Schusterman from Moscow, told me that she was deeply disappointed when they couldn't find her favorite drink, Diet Dr. Pepper, and tasked me with searching for it in St. Petersburg. Along with Yana Bruk, a community member of the foundation in St. Petersburg, we scoured the city's streets in search of the only drink that could bring a smile to her face.

Out of a desire to become part of the community, I joined "Global Shapers" of the World Economic Forum in Atlanta, a community of young people driving dialogue, action, and change by building different projects that add value to the world. The goal of the Shapers is to unite and forge connections between the world's promising leaders of tomorrow. Despite being an active member, I was informed that I wasn't listed in the association's annals because I was just over thirty when joining. Despite feeling a bit torn up about it when I found out after being involved for years, in the end, it didn't hold any real significance. At that time, through an invite of the founder Rachel Gerrol Cohen, who previously worked for Schusterman, I also joined Nexus, an organization meant to connect social entrepreneurs, people who had amassed their fortune quite young, and those who had inherited it, to form a unique network allowing authentic bonds to form. I was invited to the organization's annual event at the United Nations Headquarters in New York and would later invite several of the people I met there to Schusterman's Reality trips. Together with Narkis, I ignited the Nexus community in Israel.

Along with my many friends – among them Roi Shoshan, the brother of my friend Elad, Noga Halevi, a representative of the Jewish Agency, and Libby Novak, an expert in the world of advertising – I went on trips outside of Atlanta to Nashville and New Orleans, and spent time at TomorrowWorld, the largest electronic music festival in the world. On our ride back from a weekend at the lake, we listened to an Israeli radio station and stopped the car so we could stand on the side of the road at noon (evening time in Israel), right when Israel rang its Memorial Day siren. A passing driver stopped and offered to help. It was odd having to explain why we were standing like that in the middle of the day – quite a surreal spectacle.

For the first time in my life – and hopefully my last – I bought a car, unwillingly. You can't commute around Atlanta without one. I started with a Hyundai, and after two years I fully immersed myself in the Atlanta experience and bought a black, 328 BMW with a sunroof. I quickly learned my lesson: never buy a flashier car than your boss. This lesson, by the way, was given to me by my own boss, Seth, who half-jokingly threw in that comment.

My friend, Libby, introduced me to an amusing hobby we nearly turned into a profession: cleverly exploiting airline failures. Due to our work, we both had to fly a lot, and we soon became addicted to the airline's passenger status levels and the perks they offered accordingly. I went from silver to gold to platinum, until finally reaching the top – the coveted diamond level. It happened after a successful maneuver Libby and I cooked up after finding out that we were short just 7,000 flight points to access the prestigious club. We searched long and hard until we found a way to get there: a flight around the world to Hong Kong. We flew for 22 hours just to spend just 48 hours there, although we did scarf down a bucketload of sushi at a Michelin restaurant. We slept in a luxurious hotel (also on account of points) and flew back, right in time to be promoted to diamond level.

Libby taught me how to turn bad situations on their head, to turn disadvantages into advantages. Was your flight delayed by two hours? That's the perfect time to call the airline, rant about the important business meeting you missed, and receive hundreds of dollars in compensation. On one of my flights with Libby to London in first class (courtesy of Schusterman's golden cage) we were served frozen beets. We quickly complained and received $200 in compensation. When my suitcase didn't land in Canada, I complained and earned a shopping spree, courtesy of Delta Airlines, which included a Lululemon wardrobe renewal and a large Tumi suitcase, at the sum of around $3,000. My luggage, by the way, arrived 24 hours later.

Due to my ability to speak with nearly anyone, and evoke empathy in a variety of people (remember Aaron?) I knew how to use this to my advantage (abiding by the law, of course), to grow my bank account. My airline fun with Libby didn't prevent Delta from inviting us as guests of honor to their tour around the airline's airstrip, ending with a great dinner and a performance by John Legend.

Libby and I fooled around with the idea of launching a start-up together: a company that would deliver this service to others, meaning, one that would convert airline failures to compensation. We had no doubt this would work. If we were experiencing it, a hundred-thousand other people probably were, too, and most of them likely lacked the time to haggle with the airline's customer service. We bought a domain, built presentations, and began talking with investors. However, mainly because we were terribly busy, the idea never came to fruition.

True to the tradition of capitalizing on any situation, each time I flew out for a few days, I'd rent out my apartment on Airbnb. I have no problem with people invading my privacy – maybe because I grew up on a kibbutz – but the building I lived in didn't like the idea, and the owners threatened to kick me out of my place on several occasions. I rebelled, as I never felt I was doing something wrong. I tried looking for ways to bypass their refusal, and I eventually did. Persistence pays off.

Despite my share of success, I got my taste of failure after joining as a partner in a café called "Crema Café." Along with Roi Shoshan and the Amrani brothers (the proud sons of the founder of a famous stand in Tel Aviv's Carmel Market) I invested in a café run by another Israeli. Each of us put in $10,000 – not a crazy sum, but still substantial enough at the time – in a local place offering coffee and sandwiches. It was a self-service café with no waiters, a novel concept in those days. I liked the idea of learning how to run a new type of business, as well as grabbing a coffee at a place I owned, even though it was a 25-minute ride from where I lived.

The place flopped, to say the least. The costs were higher than expected, and the management was terrible. The experiment ended with us selling the place and losing $5,000 each. With the closing of my café, I went back to sipping on the world's largest Bloody Mary, "The Bloody Beast," at the local bar by my house. Today, by the way, Crema Café is running successfully and has even opened another branch. However, I can't credit myself for its rebound. Looking back on it today, it was the cheapest most expensive cup of coffee in my life. Lost money that wasn't trivial for me at that time, but also very cheap tuition relative to my benefit. I learned a lot about business, how important an idea is but that the execution is what counts, and I learned about the food and beverage industry and made three friends for life.

***

Despite living six years abroad, it was clear to me that my place was in Israel, and that, when the time came, I'd move back home to raise a family and continue my contribution to society from there.

Essentially, I was certain of that from the moment I stepped foot in Atlanta, and had already begun formulating a plan to get back to Israel in a matter of two-three years. I waited for the right opportunity. If I would've asked Lynn Schusterman for permission to fly back just a year into my job, she would've likely kicked me to the curb on the spot (elegantly, of course). Three years into the job, however, my situation was entirely different: I sowed the seeds, turned my role into something unique, and left a mark by leading successful journeys to Israel. I was already well-established in the foundation and had Lynn's full support and appreciation. Considering this, I felt comfortable asking for permission to continue my job in Israel.

My friend, Malvina, taught me a valuable life lesson: there are three central pillars in a person's life – their love life, workplace, and home. In times of transition, it's better to hold on to at least two of these three so as not to rock the boat too much. I knew that moving back to Israel would be difficult for me, and I made sure to make it as soft a landing as possible. I returned to my homeland with the same job I loved, and kept my same salary, which for Israel, was considered a generous sum.

I was pretty lucky when it came to finding a home. The first apartment I checked out ended up being the last one – in a run-down building in Tel Aviv, without an elevator, but overlooking the blue sea – and is the same one I live in today. My dad, sister, and her husband, David, organized it for my return. Right when I moved in, I hung pictures of two of my favorite leaders on my living room wall: David Ben Gurion and John F. Kennedy, illustrated in wacky, hippy colors.

I returned to Israel in October 2015, at the end of a Reality trip hosted for people from the Tech sector. Among the participants was the creator of Facebook's "Like" button, and the one who founded the "Code Academy." Right in the middle of our closing session in Sde Boker, my sister Leety called to tell me she was going into labor.

After saying goodbyes to the participants of the journey, I rushed to my apartment in Tel Aviv, changed my clothes, and headed to the hospital to greet my first nephew, Yoav. Or maybe it was he who greeted me on my return to Israel? Either way, this was the ultimate proof that I was in the right place. Welcome home.

My Word to the Wise

- Each one of us, especially in times of change, may go through a crisis. Try to be attentive – and no less important: figure out what helps you through it (physical exercise, meditation, a vacation, a talk with a good friend or therapist) so you can treat it before it escalates.
- Our lives comprise three central elements: our love life, work environment, and home. If you're going through a period of change, try to keep at least two of those elements stable, so as not to rock the boat too much.
- It's all a matter of timing. What seems impossible today, may very well be possible in the future. Wait for the right opportunity to act on your aspirations, and in the meantime – work towards getting there.
- Get to know your environment, and learn to love whatever you are currently doing, even if you haven't necessarily chosen it. And even if you enjoy something, make sure to notice when it's time to move on.
- We sometimes learn more from our failures then our successes. We might only realize those lessons later in life, and they will come to us in different shapes and forms, which is totally okay.

A Word to the Wise by
DORON MEDALIE, Musician,
Composer, Artistic Director

"Life is short, insist on living it."

It's the middle of the night, and I'm on the plane back from Portugal after winning the Eurovision song contest. The whole delegation is asleep, yet I'm on cloud nine, literally. I'm 40 years old, and I just won Eurovision. How insane is that? I think back on five-year-old Doron, watching Israeli singer Ofra Haza on TV perform "Chai" at the 1983 Eurovision – my first childhood memory. I'm profoundly grateful for my parents, who never once clipped my wings growing up. I've spent most of my life fulfilling my dreams, but I've met quite a few people who have had their own dreams shattered, their bright hopes and ambitions kicked to the curb.

I'm the only one awake on the plane, and I'm thinking about Mika, the young girl who approached me in the hotel, right after we won, at four in the morning. Looking up at me, she asked, "Can you teach me how to do it?"

"How to do what?"

"How do I make the things I want to happen, happen?"

"Kiddo," I chuckled, "what are you doing here?"

"I'm on a trip with my mom for my bat-mitzva."

"You're on your bat-mitzva trip, and you got to see us win the Eurovision? How fun!"

I know this moment is about to be one of the most

memorable moments in Mika's life, so I take a deep breath and reply: "If what you think and what you say and what you do are aligned, then your dreams will become reality."

This moment we shared is an accurate depiction of my whole worldview.

When you're forty, you have a wide enough perspective to reflect on your 30s and 20s. I wish someone would have told me this a few years ago.

If an angel fell from the sky right now, what would you want it to tell you? Each one of us can be someone else's angel. We've attained so much valuable insight over the years, and if we don't share it, we won't make progress.

If I would have met 20-year-old Doron, I would have told him four things:

1. 1. Get out of the closet! It's difficult, yes, but it's who you are. The burden of living a lie is so heavy, and it will only get heavier as time goes on. So, get out of the closet! Now! Enough! Each one of you has some sort of closet they're hiding in, so think about this for a few moments, and then... let's go, out with it.
2. 2. Work on your resilience. You will soon discover the harrowing effects of depression and anxiety, and while psychiatric pills may quiet some of the noise, they won't actually work in the long run. If you shut the door on your past trauma and mutter, "Everything's fine," it'll come flying back to hit you at the worst possible time in your life. Fight for the kind of life you want to live. It's all out there – all you need to do is go out and explore the healing power of herbs, the effect of music and frequencies. Move, dance, sweat, prac-

tice meditation and breathing exercises. Rediscover nature, walk barefoot, soak in the lush greenery of the forest, and pour your soul out on paper. Learn about the brain, recite mantras, find the beauty in religion if you want, whatever makes you stronger. You owe this to yourself; this world is a complete madhouse. Choose which kind of crazy you want to be.

3. There's one story floating around, one that we are all addicted to. It jumps at you from every screen, every page of the Bible, every Disney movie, and every banner you pass by without noticing. It's everywhere, so good luck with keeping your mind sane and clear. But is everyone's story your story? Don't punish yourself! Come on, start writing your own tale.

4. All cliches are true!

    Life is short, insist on living it; collect as many experiences as possible.

    Everything can be changed, everything but death.

    Troubles are plentiful; it is moments of happiness we must work to create.

    Open your eyes – love is all around.

CHAPTER 7

Tel Aviv

Journeys, Checklists, and Communities

Tel Aviv is a city of many faces. In one week, about two months after my return, I got to see two of them, one entirely different than the other.

On the one hand, my house was broken into, and at the worst possible time: on a rainy week, with a terrible leak dripping from the roof of my building, causing flooding and power outages. I found myself grieving over the stolen contents of my apartment – two cell phones, a watch I inherited from my grandfather, two passports (the biggest loss from a bureaucratic point of view), a laptop, and some cash – in a room scattered with buckets full of water dripping from the ceiling. Remember the scene from "Friends," where Chandler and Joey sit miserably in a canoe in their empty apartment? That's how I was, miserable and depressed, only with buckets instead of a canoe.

On the other hand, that same week, I was invited to play the role of Cupid to photograph a particularly exciting event at the port of Tel Aviv. Colin and Krishanti – Colin being the youngest executive director of the National Wildlife Foundation and Krishanti, his partner, who then was running for the U.S. Senate – met and fell in love on one of our "Reality" trips. Now, they were back in Israel as "facilitators" – alums who help recruit new participants and serve as leaders on "Reality Scholars," a trip intended for recipients of coveted scholarships. They decided to get engaged at the place where they first kissed, at the port of Tel Aviv, and Colin asked me to capture the memorable moment. I actually have a few spots in heaven with my name on them: at least five couples have come out of Reality trips thus far.

Apart from this touching event, the bitter taste of the robbery was further sweetened by the generosity of my exceptional boss. The following day after the burglary, I took her granddaughters, Abby and Rachel, who'd just landed in Israel, on a tour around one of Tel Aviv's famous markets. I told them about the theft, and they passed the story on to their grandmother, who kindly decided to help me. Not only was I lucky to be working in such a great place, but I was also blessed with a new, wonderful family, with everything it entailed (for better or worse).

At one of the ROI events, on the rooftop of the Mamilla Hotel in Jerusalem, Lynn Schusterman called me to the stage and presented me as a worthy candidate for all the single women (and their friends) in the crowd. It was one of those embarrassing moments that, over time, became a funny story to tell. I still enjoy watching the video that captured the event, and, unsurprisingly, made the rounds among friends.

Despite the burglary, there was no doubt that Tel Aviv, the city that couldn't have been further away from me when I was a student in Jerusalem, was now just the right fit. I was no longer a confused boy from the country, sharing an apartment on a crowded street, barely scraping by working odd gigs. With a fascinating job and a respectable salary, a diverse network of friends that was constantly growing, and an apartment overlooking the sea, Tel Aviv felt bright and right.

In the years I lived abroad, each one of my visits to Israel centered mainly around Tel Aviv, but I was a tourist back then, sleeping in hotels – a pleasant experience for one who travels light, like myself. Now, as a resident of the city, I could finally enjoy the playground spread before me. From grabbing coffee on bustling boulevards to nights out with friends I'd collected along the way – from my years as an undergrad, the ROI community, Reality journeys, and other stops – there was a lot to explore in the city. My social network, a rich and supportive community, enriched my life and opened me up to new experiences.

When I returned to Israel, in October 2015, I allocated for myself the next two to three years to work for the Schusterman Foundation, so I could gradually settle back into the country and develop professionally – before moving on to the next big thing.

One of the most captivating opportunities that came my way was when I joined the "Midburn" community, Israel's version of "Burning Man." At the heart of this eight-day festival is a temporary city peppered with caravans, tents, and mobile structures, where the goal is to create shared spaces that encourage people to flourish socially, culturally, and environmentally. Back when I lived in Atlanta, I went out with a group of Israeli friends on a fascinating caravan trip to Burning Man in Nevada – a crazy city comprising 80,000 inhabitants who set it up for no more than a week. It was a mesmerizing experience. One of the conclusions I reached following the trip was how crucial it is to make the right connections between people – let's just say that introducing Omer, an incredibly meticulous administrator, to Tomer, the Israeli version of Seinfeld's Kramer, both incredible people and close friends of mine, wasn't the best idea.

In Israel's Midburn festival, I joined Lev camp, which evolved into Bereshit, and spent eight days among a tight-knit community of people who became my family. Your camp is your home. It's where you eat, shower, and sleep – it's your grounding space during this wild week. One of the most beautiful things about our camp was the diversity of its members – hi-tech people, entrepreneurs, and musicians – which creates the right level of eclecticism, fostering wondrous experiences and a stable community.

***

My first task at hand was to find a local team to work with me on the Reality trips. This successful journey became the Schusterman Foundation's flagship program, together with its esteemed ROI program. As a matter of fact, I, myself, was the perfect example of an ROI graduate who made use of the tools and platform he received from the foundation to leverage it, step by step, to become one of the foundation's leading forces. The foundation's Israeli branch was located in Jerusalem, quite far from Tel Aviv (despite getting used to the long stretches between cities in the U.S., Jerusalem still felt lightyears away from Tel Aviv, especially when I had to commute daily). Electric scooters weren't around yet, but it was clear to me that owning a car was out of the question for now, and I felt like it would be better if my team gathered in Tel Aviv. The foundation, with its very "Jerusalem spirit," didn't want a branch in Tel Aviv, and because philanthropic foundations don't always go with what's strategically beneficial, we agreed that I'd come to Jerusalem twice a week, and the rest of the time would be spent in a shared workspace my team and I rented in Tel Aviv.

Omri Marcus, a good friend from ROI and a talented content creator, gave me a wonderful tip, similar to Libby's airline hacks. Thanks to my connections with the Carlton Hotel, which I formed by bringing in many tourist groups, they opened up their lounge for me to work in. I was happy to make use of their lavish lounge on the 14th floor of the building (right across from my apartment, which offered nothing more than a mere bowl of cereal) and hold work meetings with businessmen and politicians looking for a quiet place, far from the public eye.

Reed Hastings, founder and CEO of Netflix, says that a good CEO does not work too hard – they know how to choose the right people to do the work for them. When looking for a team – friends for the ride – I'm not afraid to recruit strong partners, ambitious and hungry, with a spark of passion in their eyes. I provide them ample space for growth and development, a fertile environment that motivates them to stay on board for a meaningful period of time.

In the lounge of the Carlton Hotel, during a meeting that would become a regular thing, I recruited Shir Marom to my team. I later brought in Natalie Hirsch, a new immigrant from Australia, who had experience working with Jewish communities around the world, and Cas Feder, a talented marketing and communications professional. By that point, I was looking for someone cool and engaging from the field of content creation in Israel to split some of the workload with me, and help create the travel itinerary. A woman named Shir, who had studied diplomacy and interned at the U.N., was the perfect fit for the job. Moreover, she was recommended to me by our mutual friend, Noga Halevi. Recommendations by friends whose opinions I value and trust is a huge plus – it says something about the candidate, but it also guarantees that good things have been said about me as well. Indeed, the first meeting with Shir seemed promising, but it also revealed an unexpected plot twist.

That same day, Noga set me up on another date: with a good friend of both hers and Shir, whom I spent a nice evening with over a bottle of wine. Shir, who was worried that her friend might have had a little too much to drink, joined us later in the evening, and eventually put an end to our date by taking her home. She was convinced, and wasn't totally wrong, that this move of hers might have cost her the job. Luckily, I got over myself and decided to hire her anyway. It was a wise decision, in every conceivable way. Shir was a loyal and professional partner every step of the way. She even took over for me once I left and remains a close friend of mine to this day. Her friend, on the other hand, ran back to the arms of the man she had been seeing before our date. And, of course, married him.

Together with my team, we grew Reality into 12 outstanding annual journeys, tailor-made for different fields of interest – wellness, sports, music, hi-tech, and more (on one of our Wellness Reality journeys, the participants gathered around for a meditation ceremony honoring my mother, while I had to visit her at the hospital after bypass surgery). In total, I spent around three months a year on the road, and I made effective use of that time to rent out my apartment on Airbnb; the sacrifice was well worth it.

Arranging these journeys was both fascinating and challenging, from the first meetings planning the itinerary and brainstorming with leading experts, to the actual execution. Together, we formulated the trip's theme: we picked out the right people, the right places, and the right connections. At the heart of each journey was the same, fundamental leadership program, only it was uniquely tweaked thanks to the different people, places, and gatherings. On the Reality Wellness trip, for example, we met with Ohad Naharin, an Israeli choreographer and the creator of the unique style of dance called "Gaga," who shared with us his methodology for a good life. On the Reality music trip, we met with Israeli musicians such as Idan Raichel, who shared deep stories about his art and his connection with the Ethiopian community.

On the Reality Sports trip, the participants were former and current athletes, Olympians and managers. Among them was Estee Portnoy, Michael Jordan's personal manager. For me, someone who desperately wanted to be Michael Jordan as a kid, it was a closure of sorts. At Doha Stadium in the Arab Israeli town of Sakhnin, members of the sports delegation met with Ahmed Abu Younes, chairman of the Sakhnin soccer team, who shared his story of being the head of the only Arab club in the Israeli Premier League. And on the shores of Sdot Yam (a kibbutz near Haifa), we met Gal Fridman, a kibbutz member, windsurfer, and Israel's first Olympic gold medalist.

On some of the trips, we met with Israel's former president, the late Shimon Peres. Meeting him was always impactful, as the elder statesman was uniquely adept at speaking to the young leaders of tomorrow standing before him.

Recruiting participants for our trips was a challenging endeavor on its own, requiring a lot of creativity and thought. During "Breakout," a meetup between entrepreneurs in Portland in a cave on the outskirts of the city, as the rain poured outside, I heard a fascinating lecture given by Colin O'Brady. Colin is the first man to have crossed Antarctica on his own, coast to coast – 54 freezing days stretched over 921 miles. I knew I had to bring him to Israel, and not only did I manage to bring him along on a Reality Wellness trip, but he later returned to the country a second time as a facilitator on Reality Sport.

Step by step, the global community of Reality alumni grew in size, reaching over 1,500 and managed by the foundation's branch in Atlanta. The goal was to preserve this growing network of people and strengthen their connections with each other, as well as their ties to Israel and the Jewish community.

I, myself, got to experience a fascinating event when I joined a cruise ship with the Summit Series community – a four-day cruise to the Caribbean, along with 3,000 entrepreneurs from different fields around the world. This delightful adventure, valued at nearly $9,000, was funded for me by the Schusterman Foundation. We set sail the day after Donald Trump was elected president. This turn of events slightly soured the mood, but the melancholy quickly dissipated. Ultimately, humans are adaptive beings, especially when surrounded by good company and great food.

I wasn't a big fan of breathing exercises before I was on a cruise and exposed to the methods of Wim Hof, a Dutch adventurist known as the "Ice Man" for his ability to withstand the freezing cold. He credits his achievements (among them, setting the world record for the longest time laying in an ice tub) to his breathing techniques. Since hearing him talk on the boat and experiencing it first hand, I am aware of the power that breathing exercises have on our minds (even though I don't practice them enough), and make sure to finish each shower with a nice stream of cold water (Ariel, my barber, says it does wonders for the hair).

***

I want to elaborate a bit on the importance of creating communities in this new, modern world, which has become quite a trend in recent years and was the focal point of my job at the time. Studies have shown that the younger generations feel far lonelier and alienated, and are looking to be part of some kind of community. This doesn't necessarily mean they're looking to go back to old, socialist kibbutz values, for example, rather, they're looking to be part of a community whose members preserve their independence. According to the dictionary definition of the word "community" in its most classic sense, a community is a group of people who share the same geographical area, values, leaders, customs, nationality, or religion within a larger population. According to my definition, a new type of community connects people with a common denominator in a way that allows them to receive from as well as contribute to the community.

There are three types of common denominators, the prevailing one being a common need. Another type of community might be predicated on a specific passion or profession. Other communities gather around a shared experience, one that doesn't necessarily have to be in person and can just as well be online, although physical meetings have proven to be more powerful.

In the words of business and management guru Prof. Henry Mintzberg: "If you want to understand the difference between a community and a network, ask your Facebook friends if they will help paint your house." We don't expect that kind of help from our Facebook friends, but from members of our community, we certainly do. Unlike a social network, communities are intimate, connected by some shared experience, one that encourages its members to give back to the people involved.

Technology allows for the expansion of our worldwide communities and certainly molds them into something else. As the years have gone by, it has become clearer that community building is a field unto itself that pays dividends – financial and otherwise. This applies to companies like Facebook and other giant corporations, which create communities around a common denominator and whose members generate profit and continuity for the organization.

Some people, like Donald Trump for example, view the world as a zero-sum game in which someone must always lose. But I believe the opposite is true and that everyone must benefit, and that is the premise on which our Reality trips were predicated. We accessed existing communities to form new ones – a win-win situation: the foundation gained a fantastic group of followers, who passed on its message to other people; the community itself earned a life-changing visit to Israel, and each of its members went through their own powerful inner journey, along with a uniting, communal one.

The timing was in our favor as well: we stood at the dawn of a new era of community building and capitalized on the opportunity. Like Aaron from the Bible, who knew how to speak to several audiences, I made good use of my skills, as well as the connections I made along the way, to reach communities that always had, surprisingly or not, a disproportionate number of influential young Jews. I'd research them and approach each one in his or her own language – forging the right connections and collaborations to reel them in. This is how the Reality community was formed, and how I became an expert at community building, and a lecturer on the topic (an endeavor that not only fascinated me but also introduced me to the love of my life... we'll talk about that in a future chapter).

The first step in building a community is knowing who you're looking for, and how they can contribute to the organization's goals and aspirations. For us, in this case, it was clear that if we could find a group of young Jews and connect them with Israel in ways that spoke to their unique characters, we'd be securing new partners for the ride. The reason you build your community in the first place should always be your guide. It's easy to veer off from your initial intention, but if it is vivid and you stick to it, it'll be easier to draw people in.

Find your potential community members by accessing the groups they are already part of. Forge partnerships and connect them with the community you aspire to form. Be sure to find precisely the right people – a few rotten apples can ruin the bunch. Your first members are those who will define the community, attract strong people to follow in their footsteps and ensure its success. For that reason, our decision to choose the Summit Series community and the influential people comprising it for our first Reality trip was crucial. It's imperative in the initial phases to generate a buzz around the community, to make some noise. Executing the first Reality journey with Noa Tishbi and Elliot Bisnow, founder of Summit Series, made a splash and created a strong desire to become a part of the community.

The community shouldn't be open to everyone, on the contrary – not everyone can be a part of it, only the select few. This was how our Reality journeys functioned: each year, only one journey flew to Israel, and only a limited number of people could join. This ensured that the community was built correctly. People understood that they had been granted access to something big and coveted, something out of reach for many people. Being part of this community automatically boosted their self-esteem. To ensure the prestige of a community, it's important to grow at a monitored pace. We could have launched 30 Reality journeys a year, but we decided to focus on 12. I participated in each one of them and upheld our value of treating each trip with the utmost attention and respect.

The goal of building a community is to establish organic growth – its members are your ambassadors. To ensure that the community you have built will keep working for you, you must do a few things. First, create a sense of belonging. This could be something small, like the water bottle I received at Harvard. It's incredible how these small gestures, whether it be a bracelet or bottle, make us feel part of something big, something we want to give back to. The second thing is creating continuity – preserve, preserve, and keep on preserving your members. Complacency is a killer. Community members have many other things on their plates, therefore, if you don't properly tend to these relationships, in a manner conducive to the goals of the community, it will fizzle. And no less important: remind the members of their shared experience. Harvard hosts several reunions, bringing back their alumni to the place it all started, reminding them that they're still a part of this institution, and in turn, encouraging them to donate and give back.

And, in conjunction with its goals and vision – important and profound as these may be – ultimately your community must also provide some fun. This hits close to home, to my worldview, in which people can succeed only when doing something they enjoy. People joined Reality trips to enjoy the shared experience, and the time they spent crisscrossing Israel together is what turned them into a true community. Creating a formative experience is one of the most important factors in building a community; it is the essence, and it is what forges the lasting bonds. A formative experience will stay with you forever and tie you to the organization, or person, who gave it to you.

***

Back to my own journey. I reached another milestone when I joined several executive boards, hoping to contribute my knowledge and experience while enriching my resume along the way. Becoming a member of an executive board is an excellent way to share your experience and vision with an organization you believe in, and in that way, help bring about change. I joined the board of The Noah Initiative, an organization that strives to find a solution to the younger generation's housing problem, and reshape the socio-economic map in Israel, and One Day Social Volunteering, a social platform bridging young people and volunteering opportunities by finding the right program fit for their availability, interests, and needs.

I'm especially honored to be part of the board of Harvard's Alumni Association in Israel. I was able to help freshen it up, in part, by forming and running The Harvard Book Prize in Israel – an award given to excelling high school students based on their academic performance, social contribution, and leadership skills, in order to encourage them to dream big. That was how I returned to my high school in the Golan Heights, alongside my former teacher, Dmitry Apartzev (who is now Katzrin's mayor) to present the award to a chosen student, Dalia Haimov. It was important for me to imbue this prize with my hopeful spirit and experience, and hand it to students whose excellence wasn't measured solely by their grades. The presentation ceremony at the mayor's office was one of the most moving moments of my life. Not only did it take me back to my childhood days in Katzrin, but it also highlighted, and made me appreciate, how far I'd come since.

Then came a fascinating new challenge, one that unfolded before me as a result of pure chance and smart utilization of the opportunity at hand. Seth Cohen was abroad, participating in an exclusive conference in Dublin, and some of the sessions were held on a train ride across Ireland. Sitting next to Seth in the car was Randall Lane, the editor-in-chief of Forbes, a Jew who hadn't visited Israel since his bar mitzvah. Among other things, Lane founded the Forbes 30 Under 30 list, an honorary list of 30 promising young people who still hadn't turned 30. Taking advantage of the opportunity, Seth who was great at spotting opportunities, invited him to speak at one of our ROI summits in Israel.

When Randall arrived, in June 2016, I was asked to show him around. We were on the roof of the SoSa complex in south Tel Aviv, overlooking the city and the sea after a wonderful night of wandering the streets and an equally splendid morning spent meeting some of the country's most fascinating entrepreneurs. As we gazed over the city, Randall confessed that he had absolutely fallen in love with Israel, particularly Tel Aviv. He later added that they were planning to host the first Forbes 30 Under 30 ceremony outside of America and were already advancing things with Paris – all they needed was one final signature – but he was now debating whether to host it in Tel Aviv.

We had no intention of missing the opportunity. Moving quickly, I pulled strings wherever I could to get things moving. I called the president's bureau and told his chief of staff that we were dealing with an urgent matter – the editor of one of the most prestigious magazines in the world was debating whether to hold an equally prestigious international summit in Paris or Tel Aviv – and that we had to strike while the iron was still hot. The following day, Seth and I sat down with Randall, in front of Israel's president, Reuven Rivlin (family ties never hurt either), who won over his heart with his charisma and homey stories of Israel and family. We also brought Lynn Schusterman into the picture, who made it happen, and invested and spread the word to several other funds. We raised half a million dollars in two days for the summit to take place in Tel Aviv. The rest is history.

Big things can happen in 24 hours, if you just push them forward: you give them a light nudge (or a strong one), act fast, and make use of all of your connections.

Forbes first international 30 Under 30 Summit lasted four days – two in Tel Aviv, two in Jerusalem – and included elements from Reality trips, such as the Mahane Yehuda Market tour. In preparation for the summit, which would include invitations to every member in the history of the exclusive 30 Under 30 club, we held a short version of the Reality trip, for a select number of those who had appeared on the list. They came united to the summit, acting as the best possible ambassadors we could have imagined. During the conference, the first list of Israel's 30 Under 30 was born, which wouldn't have occurred had the event taken place elsewhere.

Thus, thanks to the chance meeting between Seth Cohen and Randall Lane on the train, the hours we roamed with him around the country and our fast thinking, 300 Israelis, thus far, have earned a spot on this prestigious list – a stamp of honor on their resume and a catalyst for tremendous opportunity.

***

Layer by layer, I molded my work, as well as my life, into something prosperous. When I returned to Israel, my life was divided into three different parts: one-third was spent living as a bachelor in a fancy Tel Aviv apartment, another third was spent participating in Reality trips, experiencing Tel Aviv as a tourist and viewing Israel through the eyes of a foreigner, and the final third was spent abroad at summits where I fished for suitable Reality participants, and convening work meetings in the Atlanta office.

The only thing missing from my life was love (despite Lynn Schusterman's best intentions, nothing took off). While I genuinely longed for it, it seemed that my heart and brain were busy elsewhere. Tomer, my good friend, starred in a reality show called "Married at First Site," in which participants are matched up and meet for the first time at their wedding, after which they give living together a shot – all in front of the cameras. I had a minor on-screen role as the friend who threw Tomer his bachelor party and helped get him ready on the big day. I grew close to the directors and decided to audition for the show's second season.

Ultimately, I didn't need the show's matchmakers and TV cameras to help me find love. If there's one thing life has taught me, it is that everything has its own time.

My Word to the Wise

- Reacting quickly to a situation is oftentimes crucial. Know when to strike, and tackle it with all of your might.
- Make use of social connections to find a job or locate employees – people who know both sides well are the best matchmakers.
- Don't be afraid to hire strong employees – look for those who are hungry for success and full of passion. Give them the space to grow and develop.
- Communities can be a valuable part of your life. Find (or create) the right one for you to flourish.

A Word to the Wise by
NARKIS ALON,
Social Entrepreneur

*"What sparks your curiosity enough
for it not to feel like a job?"*

My first serious job was at a start-up, where I developed its business model and sales. While most of my friends were waitressing, I was meeting marketing executives, trying to sell our product. Truly proud of myself, I felt like I was on the right path to a successful career.

But in truth, most of the time I was terribly anxious. My mood depended on my boss's opinion of me. If he was happy, I was happy. If he criticized my work, I took it to heart and cried. I was sure that's what it meant to be a working adult.

When I traveled after my military service, I came to the realization that this job wasn't for me, and that I was missing a sense of meaning, which could be realized by serving a higher cause. The last time I felt fulfillment was in a youth movement, and I believed that if only I did something to serve others, I'd recreate that same feeling.

Upon my return to Israel, I co-founded an organization called "ZeZe" (This is It). Along with my partners, we created projects that bred job opportunities for underprivileged communities. Most of these projects were led by students, who, through jobs obtained here, gained valuable experience in fields of their interest.

Even though forming this organization was exciting, I continued to suffer from extreme mood swings. I was constantly concerned about our projects and was often sick. After a few years, I decided it was best to move on. When I wondered why I couldn't stick to this job as well, I concluded that the issue was probably money. Our organization was a non-profit, and as we struggled to raise funds, we were left without a proper paycheck. I was desperate to leave my parents' house and live independently, so I decided that my next endeavor would combine both the social and business worlds – the best of both worlds.

And so it was. Along with a partner of mine, I founded an academy training people interested in working in hi-tech. We managed to make a proper living, as well as contribute to our society – our courses were meant for those coming from underprivileged backgrounds. I was working with investors, a remarkable team of employees, and partnering with major hi-tech companies. Yet it was in that period of my life, in that particular workplace, that I suffered the most. I was constantly exhausted, stressed, frustrated, and far from my romantic partner and my circle of friends.

At this point, I was confused: no matter which way I looked at it, this time, I was supposed to be happy. This job had everything – money, meaning, status in the local start-up field, and was full of challenges – yet I felt entirely disconnected from myself.

At the age of 27, when I realized I had to quit but didn't know how or where to go, I met with many people who were as confused as I was about their career paths and asked them questions to help them through it. In that way, I hoped to gain some insight about myself as well. I noticed that there was one question that brought out the most clarity in people: "Describe what your daily routine would look like in your ideal job." Their answers were diverse. They described the kind of people they'd meet, the way their office looked, and how much money they'd make. But the main thing they discussed was their daily workload: whether they'd be asked to write documents, solve problems, lecture in front of an audience, manage projects, sort out funds, sell products, brainstorm in meetings, do administrative work, or a little bit of everything.

When I asked myself that same question, the picture began clearing up: none of the activities of my dream job had to do with what I'd been doing in recent years. The things I genuinely enjoyed doing were done in my spare time. I gave them the lower rank of "hobbies," while most of my day was spent doing things I didn't quite like. The story I'd tell people was always very impressive in theory: "creating work opportunities for people in need," "training people to work in hi-tech" – but in reality, as I was accomplishing all these things, I wasn't doing what I enjoyed.

When listening to lectures given by successful leaders,

I'd always hear them talk about their initial goal and the challenges they managed to overcome, how they beat the odds. But no one ever talked about simply... enjoying oneself along the way. By looking inward, I realized that I genuinely love talking to people and asking them questions. I love writing and helping people undergo transformational processes. I love speaking in front of audiences and dreaming big with my colleagues. All these became the focal points of my current career.

Nowadays, I run workshops on women's leadership in organizations, academic institutions, and within the projects I lead, including "DoubleYou," and my podcast, "Playing with Fire," where I discuss the relationship between women and men. I also write content for "Fortune 500" and various academic institutes in Israel. I've recently published the book "Alive Women," and I consistently write and interact with my followers. Most importantly: I create and make a living by doing what I love the most.

Bottom line: Don't be blinded by grandiose titles and stories. Think about yourself as if you were still a kid: What sparks your curiosity enough for it not to feel like a job? What comes naturally enough so you can stick with it when times get tough? What would you want to do, even if you knew you might fail at it? Go for it.

In the words of Israeli musician, Berry Sakharof: "Don't wander far, stay near. That is what it means to love yourself."

CHAPTER 8

Between Silicon Valley and Ben-Gurion Boulevard

Just the right timing, even for love

My job was a golden cage, made of pure, glistening gold. I had no reason to complain: it was interesting, fun, and challenging. With the help of a great team, I continued to build and expand the Reality trip recruitments, running 12 annual journeys that saw great success. My work was greatly appreciated and commended, which was duly reflected in my salary. But deep down, something was stirring.

A good friend once told me that five years in the same job is the right time to move on. The first year is a bit chaotic, the two years that follow are ones of growth and change, the fourth year starts feeling repetitive, and the fifth is just the right time to go looking for the next big thing. Of course, this isn't true for every job and depends on the state of your career, but I agree with the general idea. The time comes when, after doing the same job repeatedly, one needs to ask oneself whether one is still learning something new, and that's where I was.

All things considered, it's very hard to leave one's comfort zone, especially if it's perfectly cushioned, as was mine. It's hard to step away when we feel in our element. We start to think that our specific "reality" is all there is to life. I, for one, was completely immersed in the foundation and Reality journeys, which, to me, felt like the center of the universe. It's hard to look beyond our narrow horizon and see the big picture and the immense potential just off in the distance.

The golden cage is so comforting and pampering that the easiest thing to do is just cuddle up inside and never once look outside. The first step toward moving from this tricky place is admitting to yourself that you're slightly addicted to this comfort and that it may be time to part ways and move on.

In some paradoxical way, the generous gift I received from the Schusterman Foundation was what also served as my wake-up call.

***

The first time I heard about Singularity University was while working on a tech-themed Reality trip with Daniella Segal, a good friend who worked at a company developing virtual reality. Some of the participants of this specific trip were graduates of the institution and shared wonders about this great Californian university.

The Singularity University, which works in collaboration with the International Space University and whose partners include Google, NASA, LinkedIn, and others, is located at the joint civilian-military airport, Moffett Field, in Silicon Valley (once a NASA center). Its mission: "To create, teach, and inspire future leaders striving for knowledge, and to utilize technology as a means for solving some of humanity's biggest challenges." In simpler terms: they seek to understand where the world is heading and how to get there.

The university is meant to supplement other existing academic institutions and accepts (via a strict admissions process) graduates who had already done a thing or two in their lives. The various study tracks, ranging from a few days to several months, focus on subjects like innovation, funding and business entrepreneurship, virtual reality, nanotechnology, artificial intelligence, space science, neuroscience, public policy, and ethics. These topics are all taught by leading experts, all pioneers in their respective fields.

My first step while applying to this prestigious program was ensuring some way to fund it. It's a very expensive track: over $10,000 for five days! I took the initiative and together with Seth, proposed that the Schusterman Foundation fund professional development for its employees, spearheading a policy that conveniently enough offered senior employees a sum of $10,000. I made sure that Singularity University fit this criterion perfectly: not only would it add to my professional development, but it would also expand the circle of candidates for our Reality trips. It would be a great way of getting familiar with this new world we hoped to offer them. Therefore, I didn't hold back from asking them to fund my studies. I knew Lynn Schusterman would agree to do it if I'd get her to see how beneficial it was for the foundation, much like the way I convinced people to purchase Dead Sea products back at the mall in Canada – I wasn't lying to them by guaranteeing a good product, and they were the ones who decided to buy it. Eventually, the foundation agreed to fund my studies, including a round-trip flight to California.

In October 2017, I flew to Silicon Valley for five days of pure fascination and awe – a glimpse into the "new world." I studied with senior executives from all over the world, among them, the CEO of JPMorgan Chase Bank in Brazil, as well as one other Israeli – Gil Sheratzki, Ituran's Chief Business Development Officer, who instantly became a good friend of mine thanks to the Israeli sense of humor we both shared. We heard intriguing lectures by global experts, who shared their views on where the world is heading. We visited innovative companies around Silicon Valley and dealt with questions about some of the world's future challenges, for example, how will Africa look in ten years, where will professionals whose jobs might soon become extinct work (for example, drivers who will be replaced by autonomous cars), and what kind of effect blockchain technology will have on our lives (I still haven't invested enough).

Those five days in Silicon Valley got me thinking about my next phase in life. At Singularity, there was a lot of talk about exponential growth – a rapid and unrestrainable growth rate, measured by multiples – unlike linear growth, which is a careful, measured progression advancing in a straight line. The world is progressing exponentially, and whoever wants to be on top of things must be a part of this growth. In terms of the foundation, after contributing to its exponential stage (400% growth rate over two years), I realized that I was stuck on the linear plain – there was no more room for development. I needed to embark on a new path and find my next exponential station: a place that was moving forward quickly and changing the world through new technology. At the time, I never could have imagined that my next station would perfectly fit this description.

On the 31st of January 2018, after an emotional farewell party at a nice restaurant in Jaffa, during which my colleagues played a game of "Who Knows Yaniv Better" and showered me with tons of love, I said goodbye to the Schusterman Foundation, which, for me, was more than a workplace: it was family.

I was confident in my decision, but was concerned nonetheless: What if no one wants me out there? Will I ever get a job as lucrative and gratifying as this one? Are the skills and experience I gained over the years enough to land me my next big thing? Still, I spread my wings and parted from my cushy nest into the unknown, with a general idea of where I was heading.

One of the most important things when faced with a crossroads in life is to build yourself a proper schedule: define how much time you can afford to look around before you start working again. Take your financial situation and other aspects into consideration (for example, not everyone will enjoy a year of unemployment, even if they can afford it financially). When you define how much time you have, it's easier to enjoy laying idly on the beach, a treat you rightfully deserve, knowing that in two months, you'll be back in the workforce.

I set myself a period of six months, which began a day after I left the foundation, on the enchanting shores of Thailand. Recommended to me by friends, I went to "The Sanctuary" on the southern island of Koh Pha-ngan, which, as its name states, is a temple of pure and serene leisure. I drifted between restorative retreats, refreshing massages – one of my favorite treats in the world – and hanging out on the shore, gazing out at the azure waters with a coconut in one hand and a book in the other, the perfect Instagram picture for the Thailand tourist (to complete the cliché, the book I was reading was "Transitions" by William Bridges, who discusses the three stages an individual experiences during change: Ending What Currently Is, The Neutral Zone and The New Beginning).

From Thailand, I flew to Mexico City to meet with Isaac Lee, Juan's partner, a friend I met on a Reality trip. Isaac was one of the senior executives at Univision Communications, a major media corporation, the largest one in Spanish – it has over 60 television channels, a cable network, and various apps. Isaac and I brainstormed about my next job, one that would be tailored specifically to my competence and skills, such as a role as his chief of staff. I took advantage of the luxurious hospitality he provided, which included an overnight stay at the Four Seasons Hotel, to meet with some friends in Mexico. Among them was Lilia, one of the Israeli Trek participants, who, while studying at Harvard, also ran for Congress and won. And Alberto Dana, a Mexican Jew, Reality alumni and entrepreneur who became a dear friend and, at the same time, happened to organize a remarkable experience around Mexico City to introduce it to his friends from abroad.

Isaac's offer was as tempting as it was challenging – an opportunity to learn about an industry completely new to me, in a foreign country, from one of the top experts in the field – and it had both positive and negative aspects to it. Eventually, the offer never fully ripened. Isaac left the company two months after we met. As usual, it's all a matter of timing, and this was probably not the right time for me to leave Israel and move to Mexico. Our lives are filled with alternating, sliding doors ("Sliding Doors" starring Gwyneth Paltrow is one of my all-time favorite movies), and I often found myself wondering where that particular door would have led me.

During this "in-between" phase, I engaged with my diverse network of acquaintances. When looking for a job, it's best to first talk to those closest to you, with whom you can consult without the fear of being judged, who know you best and can help clarify your goals and offer the right kind of connections to get you to the right people. With your close friends, you can afford to be a bit lost and confused. It's just the right environment to brainstorm amid this confusion. However, the moment you move on and meet with people they connected you with, you have to get your act together and be as focused and resolute as ever, because no one will do the work for you.

This valuable tip was given to me by Jordan Ormont,

a Reality alum and then a senior talent partner at one of the world's leading venture funds, and whose wise words I convey to every young person approaching me for professional advice. I could afford to ponder aloud with Juan, but the moment he sent me to Isaac, I was already switched on. If you arrive at a meeting all confused with someone who has carved out time especially to help you find a job, not only will you be wasting his time (and yours), you might come off as seriously unprofessional and squander the generous opportunity you were given. If you show up centered and collected, it'll be easier for the person to help you and make the right connections.

After a long period of deep conversations with people close to me from different sectors, my next venture in life was starting to come together: my vision was of a workplace providing experience in the business world, but one that wouldn't be purely business. It was clear to me that my next role would have to be socially significant and impactful. This added value – an integral part of my agenda – is what helps me flourish, succeed, and do good in the world.

While the picture did indeed brighten up, it was still somewhat vague. The goal I set for myself could be accomplished in various fields, and this ambiguity kept me nervous and worried about not finding what I was looking for. Naturally, the moment I shifted from my comfort zone and opened up, the world itself opened up in return. The reputation I established for myself and the connections I formed worked like magic. A stream of offers came flowing my way, each one unique and interesting in its own right. Among them were offers from the field of real estate, an offer to serve as the CEO of an Israeli start-up company working on education, an offer to establish with a group of friends a start-up investing in people (for example: investing in funding the studies or research of promising people in exchange for future profits), as well as an offer to establish a new study program at Reichman University's Lauder School of Government, Diplomacy and Strategy.

It was exciting to swim in this sea of possibilities. I learned a lot, and people's belief in me certainly boosted my ego. The fact that people were offering me all these tempting proposals strengthened my confidence, which can be fractured when stepping out of one's comfort zone. At that point, it hit home that we don't know what we don't know and that there are multiple realities out there (no pun intended), and that only by stepping outside of our comfort zone, we can become more exposed and learn things that we couldn't have imagined existed.

During that time, I continued lecturing in different places on the power of communities. One of the companies I was invited to was the Israeli start-up Jolt, which offers alternative study programs for business management degrees on campuses it established in Israel and worldwide. I was a member of the company's advisory committee, which assisted in putting together a program to train business management students in different methods relating to hi-tech, providing an alternative route to an MBA.

Before one of my talks, at Tel Aviv's Jaffa Port, I was approached by a woman named Ofir Charlap, who also works in "reality," but of a different kind – "Reality" is the name of the largest group of real estate funds in Israel. Ofir and I hung out in similar circles and knew each other a bit from before, and after a pleasant conversation, I asked her if she wanted to grab a coffee later on. The lecture I gave went well, and the meeting with Ofir afterward was even better.

Ofir came into my life and into my heart at just the right time, when I was mentally free for it – shortly after leaving the Schusterman Foundation and a while before the future revolution of BIRD. I decided to give the budding romance a chance and gave up my initial intention to participate in the "Wedding at First Sight" reality show. It's certainly possible that it was pure chance that brought us both together that spring morning on March 23, 2018, for a lecture at Jaffa Port. Either way, ever since I asked Ofir out for that cup of coffee, I've been preparing her one each morning, and I plan on doing so for the rest of my life.

***

A month later, in April, the events played out – or better put: unfolded – at a dizzying pace. I met Sam Rozen, a successful entrepreneur, on a Reality Tech trip, the one that ended on the day I returned to Israel for good. And on one of his visits here, he offered me the opportunity to join one of his companies to generate clean water and make it accessible to all. We met at a bar and sat facing the boulevard, bustling with bikes and scooters. Sam asked if I had heard of the company BIRD, which was founded in Los Angeles three months prior by Travis VanderZanden. "I believe," he said, "they're looking for ways to expand." I Googled the company and read about its creation of shared e-scooters. I told Sam this could definitely work in Israel, particularly in Tel Aviv – a congested city whose residents had already begun riding private scooters anyhow.

As we discussed the matter over a cup of coffee on the boulevard, Sam emailed Paige Craig, a friend of his who worked at BIRD. Paige connected me with Patrick Studener, BIRD's only employee working outside the U.S., in Amsterdam, whose job was to ignite and spearhead the company's international market. We had a few calls on Zoom – way before COVID made it a household name – and Patrick asked that I prepare a quick market analysis. I did a lot of reading and researching, and truthfully, it was quite easy to convince them of the immense potential e-scooters had in Tel Aviv. E-scooters had already landed in Israel in 2016, so the city was already open to the idea (unlike other places in the world, where private e-scooters weren't on the streets before BIRD came along). Tel Aviv, a city of only 480,000 inhabitants, welcomes over one million cars daily and is the most congested in the OECD. It is always desperate to find solutions to its traffic and parking problems. Israelis are early adopters, and Israel as a start-up nation is naturally open to innovation. And the weather here is perfect for riding scooters nearly all year long.

Competing job offers increase your value, each one prodding and motivating the other. And as for your part in reaching a decision, I believe in this determining question: What would you like to talk about during Friday night dinner? At this laid-back evening at the end of a long week, whether spent with family or friends, all of your deliberations materialize because it is around that table that your real passion comes to light. Even after all the brainstorming, meetings, thoughts, and interviews, you are the only one who knows what you're truly passionate about, and the only one who can answer the question of what really matters to you and makes you tick. Do you want to hold a secondary position at a top company, or create something new for yourself? Would it bother you if your good friend was your boss or business partner? Do you believe in the product?

The answers to all these questions, and many more, shed light on where I wanted to be and helped filter out offers that weren't aligned with my passion. The chance to be part of BIRD felt perfectly in line with my aspirations (even though many people warned me that it wouldn't succeed: Israelis wouldn't want to pay for this service, and the scooters would be vandalized or stolen on day one, and in any case, why would someone want to share a scooter if they could have one of their own? The chance to be head of my own kingdom in Israel, to start something from scratch, revolutionize the country's transportation sector, gain business experience in a forward-thinking company, enjoy all that these converging worlds had to offer, and combine business success with a revolutionary business model while bringing about social change – it all appealed to me. Of course, all of this was a double-edged sword. This would be my first time establishing such an operation, I had never run a company of this size before, and if the City of Tel Aviv rejects my plan, everything will collapse before it even has a chance to begin.

I took a risk by joining a new company in a field I wasn't experienced in. However, it was a calculated one. What was the worst that could happen? At most, I would have found out that it wasn't for me, and I would have moved on. In this case, I would have gained experience from simply trying. Any way I looked at it, the pros outweighed the cons. Everyone must calculate their own risk-reward ratio. The way I viewed it, BIRD was a blend of entrepreneurship with the well-paying salary of a company employee.

What did I have to lose? I didn't see this project failing by any means. I mean, our world is changing at a crazy speed. A decade ago, who would have dreamed that we'd be sharing apartments and transportation? Today, this shared economy is an inseparable part of our day-to-day lives. To be the first to jump on this wagon, one needed to take risks. When everybody is telling you, "no, no, no," you know you are on the right path (although it helps to have a few "yesses" along the way!). As Henry Ford once said, "If you had asked most people what they wanted, they would have said, 'faster horses.'" It's hard for most people to envision revolutions, which is why they are revolutions.

On the night between the 19th and 20th of April, Ofir and I joined our friends, Eitan and Neta, to celebrate their loving relationship in the desert. A little after midnight, at the start of my birthday, at more or less the hour I was born 36 years ago, I looked at my phone and saw a message flickering on my screen from Patrick:

"Yaniv, just got off the phone with Travis. In short, we want to do Israel ASAP, and hopefully, you're the man to do it. Call me when you have a second."

My Word to the Wise

- Ask yourself, and be honest: do you feel like you've exhausted your current place in life? Do you feel like you have nowhere else to grow and develop? Have you been doing the same thing repetitively for a while now? If your answer is "yes," this is probably the time to leave your comfort zone and look for new challenges.
- When you're in between jobs, set a timeframe for yourself. This will allow you to enjoy your time off without feeling guilty about it and will tell you when it's time to get serious again and find something new.
- Ask good friends for help, those who know you well and will do everything they can to help you. Brainstorm with them and use this space to refine and specify your goals. With their help, find the right connections to move you forward.
- Examine your job offers from all angles and decide which is best for you. For example: does it feel right to work with close friends? Would you rather secure yourself a spot at a top company, or lead your own venture?
- It's easier to enjoy a job when you connect with its values. Think about this when you choose your next workplace. Ask yourself: what would you want to talk about at dinner with family and friends? The topic that comes up is the right choice for you.
- We don't know what we don't know. Once we step outside of our comfort zone, we can see the multiple realities that are out there and get to know and learn things that we couldn't have imagined.

A WORD TO THE WISE FROM
OFIR CHARLAP RIVLIN,
IMPACT AND INNOVATION ENTREPRENEUR IN REAL ESTATE

"Grab a cup of coffee with someone interesting. Who knows, you might end up marrying them."

There are times in life when we find ourselves at a crossroads. I, for one, remember feeling overwhelmed by everything the world has to offer. How does one choose? "Grab a coffee with people from different backgrounds and ages," my brother advised me during that uncertain time. "Listen to how they introduce themselves and only then share your story." I decided to follow his advice and asked him to connect me with people he appreciates, adding some of my own to the list.

He connected me with Asaf Vardi, an incredible man and a partner at "Reality," the largest real estate investment fund in Israel. We spoke about dreams and aspirations, and how people create new and improved realities in places that were once gray and are now brimming with life. I also met Lior Suchard, an Israeli mentalist who had worked with several partners to create the biggest "escape room" in the Middle East, a blooming trend at the time. We talked about creating an experiential, stimulating, and unique space. I continued my coffee dates with entrepreneurs, designers, architects, artists, people from hi-tech and real estate, family members and friends, as well as with myself. I asked to hear their life story and later shared my own. Through those conversations, it became clear that what I wanted to do in life was make a living out of doing good in the world. Back then, there wasn't a name for it, but today, we call it "impact" – comprising two bottom lines of profit: economic and social-environmental.

As time went on, my social network grew and fascinating opportunities started coming my way – from forming shared workspaces to novel hangout spots to start-ups teaching and developing future professions. I began to understand my dreams and others' dreams – and how to achieve them.

What interested me was creating spaces that delivered a meaningful experience. I wanted to take part in the formation of companies that have an added social value, that will serve as fertile ground for people's dreams to come true – from the initial idea to its planning, all the way to its execution. In essence, I wanted to do this with people I love and care for.

That was how I joined the wondrous team of people working on creating an "escape room," followed up by another adventure – building an international community in Brazil at the Rosemary Dream, and finally, finding a spot at "Reality." The transition from a dreamy position in Brazil to Israel's real estate field led me to dive deeper into what my dreams and those of other people were, and how we could achieve them. I was lucky enough to join a team of talented partners to develop the impact and innovation aspect of real estate. Together, we turned old commercial centers into bright and animated shared spaces encouraging cultural, artistic, and social development. Places where NGOs, businesses, authorities, and local communities could connect. We combined unique content with a social outlook – the environmental angle alongside economic growth. I now understood, firsthand, what Abraham Lincoln meant when he said: "The best way to predict the future is to create it." What began in 2017 with a series of 40 coffee dates, became my life's engine and driving force for social progress.

At the start of 2018, at a conference discussing the importance of community building, I met Yaniv Rivlin, who spoke about the Schusterman Foundation's Reality trips. Both of us were developing realities of our own. And, as per my newfound custom, we concluded our brief talk at the conference with a plan to meet for coffee afterward. Three days later, we met again over coffee. And, lo and behold, it didn't stop there. To this day, I go out for coffee with new people, and to my delight, we work on turning dreams into reality.

So, how does one turn their dream into reality?
- **By wearing a smile** – Because when you act from a place of good intentions, good things will likely come from it.
- **By dreaming** – Everything starts with a dream.
- **By being bold** – Just try. At most, you'll get a "yes." Once you try, you open up the possibility for things to happen.
- **By making the right connections** – Ones that help us fulfill our dreams. Many of the initial connections I made didn't bear immediate fruit. Things ripened and matured over time. Suddenly, interesting offers began to come my way, fruitful partnerships, fascinating projects, and inspiring relationships.

CHAPTER 9

From a Bird's Eye View

A Revolution Brought About
by Two Wheels and a Board

I landed the role of BIRD's GM (General Manager) in Israel over three bottles of Rosé at a bar above one of Amsterdam's canals. Today, in light of the intricate and rigid process of getting accepted into the company, I'm not sure I would succeed in landing such a senior position. One thing's for sure: with the resume I had back then, I wouldn't have hired myself for the job. But all the circumstances worked in my favor: I was at the right place at the right time. To my credit, I can say quite proudly that I was able to identify these opportunities and make the most of them.

I spent the weekend of my 36th birthday, right after the message I got from Patrick Studener, celebrating with my family in the north of Israel. On Sunday, I was already on a plane to Amsterdam, off to my first in-person meeting with Patrick, funnily enough, on *his* birthday, for a week that would change my life – and by no small measure, the face of Tel Aviv as well.

Patrick was an Austrian who had previously worked at Uber, where he met Travis VanderZanden, BIRD's CEO and founder. He stayed in Amsterdam due to work and was living in the city with his girlfriend, Eva. Only in retrospect, I learned that in order to get the job, I had to pass her test as well. Fortunately, the chemistry between all of us was instant.

Patrick's birthday celebrations that week were spent meeting and working with me at cafes around Amsterdam. By that point, BIRD had already expanded from Los Angeles to a few cities around the U.S. and was looking for markets in Europe. Legend has it that the idea of e-scooters and solving the "last mile" problem – getting from the bus stop to the passenger's final destination – sprung from Travis' childhood, during which he would occasionally join his mom, who worked for 30 years as a bus driver in Wisconsin.

A pioneer in its field, BIRD became one of the major players in the shared e-scooter market and took the world by storm at a dizzying speed. During its first fundraising round, it raised $15 million, in the second $100 million, and in the third round, which was signed in June 2018 – two months before the company's launch in Israel – it raised $300 million, led by Sequoia Capital, one of the most respected venture capital firms in Silicon Valley. I came at just the right time.

I'm not ashamed to say that transportation problems weren't keeping me up at night before hearing about

BIRD, and I didn't walk around feeling like I was the one who had to fix them. In fact, I had never ridden an electric scooter before (today I'm constantly riding them). That being said, I instantly felt drawn to the company's vision: revolutionizing transportation with shared e-scooters that may potentially lead to fewer cars on the road, and in turn, ease the city's traffic jams and lessen its air pollution. The more I looked into the company, the more I saw its huge potential.

I came to Amsterdam with the right cards in hand: I already had some interesting job offers up my sleeve, therefore, Patrick was the one who had to convince me to join their expanding company and build its first brand outside the U.S. I enjoyed working with him in Amsterdam and quickly concluded that this was the place for me – a global company with a bright future, as its first GM outside of the U.S., dealing with the enthralling challenge of building a market and global playbook from scratch.

Even so, as per the rules of the game, I still played hard to get. The financial conditions offered to me were an upgrade from my previous job, albeit not to a large extent. In the hi-tech world, unlike philanthropy and public services, one is handed a dream in the form of stock options. When I left Amsterdam, I didn't give Patrick the sense that I was fully in. I expressed just the right amount of enthusiasm as well as caution. We parted ways as friends and agreed to have him prepare the contract for me to go over.

I returned home excited. Things seemed to be moving in the right direction. Needless to say, I turned down the initial contract with the aim of improving it. I was walking down the streets of Tel Aviv when Travis called to tell me that he'd heard great things about me and that he'd be happy to have me join. As I walked along the boulevard of a city I planned on revolutionizing, Travis and I examined Israel's potential in integrating this form of transportation. A few days later, when Patrick called to say they accepted all of my conditions, or in other words, "Come on, let's do this," I was at another wedding. I had a good reason to go wild on the dance floor.

***

I also had good reason (in fact, very good) to be worried. With all due respect to the experience and skills I had acquired along the way, my toolbox was certainly lacking. Every person who was hired further on down the road to serve as the GM of other BIRD markets was either an MBA graduate or one with sufficient experience managing similar operations. The experience I had was in a completely different field, but the network of people I'd connected with through the Reality trips upgraded my reputation. Mike Basch, a Reality alum and a mutual friend of both of ours had good things to say about me to Patrick. Let this serve as more proof of the importance of excelling in whatever you do along the way because that will serve as your diploma, allowing you to maneuver between fields (by the way, one of the guest attractions at Mike's wedding, held in Israel, was an iconic evening trip along Tel Aviv's boardwalk riding BIRD's e-scooters).

The right place for me was one where I could make a change. Fortunately, many fields offered that. In the "old world," employees were considered "special experts" – experts at one thing only. Back then, it made sense to start your career at a bank and leave that same bank 40 years later. Of course, there's nothing objectively wrong with that, and this may still suit some people, but in our new world, we have the opportunity to challenge ourselves and transition across fields to find the place we blossom the most. In this world, those who flourish are "generalists" – people who, unlike "experts," have the right set of skills to work in a multitude of fields (like me). The role of GM demanded I know a bit about everything, but it didn't require that I become proficient in one specific area.

I had most of the skills required for the job – the ability to read situations and examine the stakeholder map, the ability to think ahead, to create a vision with specific goals, sketch an outline on how to achieve them, the ability to get along with people, and a crazy level of ambition. All of this, in addition to my vast experience working in different fields. However, there were also many things missing from my resume, such as experience in leading a company, and experience in building such an operation from the ground up. This, of course, gave rise to many concerns about my chances of succeeding in the job. I pushed through many challenging moments, but I had no intention of revealing this to my employers. This was precisely the time to embrace and implement the good old "fake it 'till you make it" mantra. This doesn't mean that you're completely faking it, just that you need to try and present things with confidence at critical points in your career. Know how to tell your story so that everything that you did will stand to your credit. This is precisely what I did.

Apparently, we did something right, because a while after I joined BIRD, it reached "unicorn" status – a private company worth a billion dollars, the fastest such valuation in history – only eight months after it was founded. Airbnb, for example, reached that status after 36 months.

***

I spent the last couple of days before stepping into this new role (we were busy with legal matters integrating the company in Israel) with my camp members at the "Midburn" festival. Nature is a comfortable and truly recommended setting for contemplating future decisions. Unlike my mom, who wondered if the reason I went to Harvard was to run a scooter company, my friends thought the idea was quite cool.

Amid all these events, I managed to work on one of my favorite undertakings: connecting between worlds. I helped Forbes, and its editor, Randall Lane – by this point, we were already referring to each other as "mishpocha" (family) – to enlist sponsors for its 30 Under 30 conference in Israel. I brought in my friend from Katzrin, Roy Peled, to help out. Roy was known to the public as the boyfriend of Lee Zitoni, a 25-year-old who died in a hit-and-run accident in 2011, and the man who fought to bring the reckless drivers, who later fled to France, to justice. Randall wanted Israeli model Bar Refaeli to participate in the conference, so we got a meeting with her mother Tzipi, who connected us with Yossi Gabison-Sasa, the owner of major apparel brands Hoodies and Carolina Lemke, which Bar modeled for.

The meeting was held at a café at the port of Tel Aviv and was tremendously successful. Carolina Lemke, which was looking to break into the American market, sponsored the conference and handed out sunglasses to all of its participants. At this festive event, Roy shared his special story, and Randall Lane interviewed Bar Refaeli (and I got to dance on the tables in Jerusalem's Mahne Yehuda Market with one of my childhood heroes, NBA star Amar'e Stoudemire).

Randall, on his end, used his network to connect Carolina Lemke and Kim Kardashian, who became the brand's model abroad. I won some perks as well: I was invited to watch the closing event of the Giro d'Italia at a luxurious penthouse of billionaire Sylvan Adams (who is responsible for bringing the prestigious cycling tournament to Israel) along with other guests, including Bar Refaeli and Tel Aviv's mayor, Ron Huldai. The timing was excellent: Patrick, who also came to Israel for a visit, went along with me and was impressed by my abundant network. Since then, I have been coined "The Mayor" at BIRD.

Thus, all of my worlds connected – from Katzrin to Reality trips, to Forbes to BIRD – in the best possible way. Connecting different worlds is crucial to getting ahead, but you must know when and how to do it. Each connection needs to be done accurately, and not simply for the sake of making a connection, because an unsuccessful meeting can create distress for the parties involved and greatly tarnish your reputation. Proper utilization of your social network to create successful bonds is good karma in this world and manifests great things. Such connections have the power to produce a result greater than the sum of their parts. Having good emotional intelligence helps one understand whether the people, who presumably have the right skills to work together, will actually get along. As in the capital market, the same leverage can be produced in the human market, in this case, by connecting people.

A second before I dove into a world that was all about e-scooters, I managed to fly to New York for a short visit, after joining a class action lawsuit against Yahoo due to a security breach that affected the accounts of all its users – around three billion users. The lawsuit was filed by a fellow HKS alum who was looking for two Israelis who were affected and would agree to join. And so, attorney Mali Granot and I found ourselves, together with our spouses, flying first class to New York to testify (and paint the town red). After all, Robin Hood deserved a little something for a testimony that helped yield $117.5 million in compensation, distributed among the complainants. Without the Israeli witnesses, no one in Israel would have received any money.

Upon my return, I pulled up my bootstraps and got to work, without fanfare, building something from nothing. Much was at stake. We didn't want BIRD's expected arrival in Israel to leak at this early stage, so as not to give our competitors any ideas or scare off cities whose cooperation we would need – and also, to maintain the momentum. I didn't change my title on LinkedIn and recruited people discreetly. I held work meetings with Patrick and Sam, who was sent from the company's headquarters to help me launch the business, from my apartment, which, for a long while, was not only my private address but also the company's official address in Israel. We worked from home, in a start-up atmosphere par excellence, long before COVID made working from home a given. Only later did we settle into the accelerator DRIVE TLV in south Tel Aviv – a center for innovation focusing on smart, mobile solutions – after my friend from "Ituran" connected me with DRIVE's founders. We caused a bit of havoc in the center, but everyone who visited that office loved our e-scooters.

I flew to BIRD's headquarters in Venice Beach to get to know the company, which, back then, had no more than 200 employees. Excited as ever, I walked into the office and saw all the swag – shirts, hats, bottles with wings on them (remember, branding is imperative, it creates a sense of connection with the product). I was thrilled to take part in the BIRD Fam – the headquarters' weekly all-hands meeting – and take my first scooter ride along Venice Boulevard, knowing that I was part of this pioneering venture. In L.A., as would happen in Tel Aviv later on, the scooters were dispersed throughout the city without obtaining prior permission from city hall. Legend has it that Travis and the first couple of employees placed the first ten scooters on the sidewalk and hid behind the bushes to see if people would use them. The success was immediate. At times, you just have to establish facts on the ground.

My first ride on an electric scooter happened right after I was hired as BIRD's GM. Along with my friend Omer, I purchased my own scooter. Up to that point, I had commuted mainly by taxi. While the first ride on the scooter was a bit frightening, I immediately spotted its potential, and now, I can't picture my life without it. I was even given the title of the company's MVBF (Most Valuable Bird Fammer), being the employee with the most BIRD rides around the world. This is the reason why I'm so excited about my job – the product I'm selling, which wasn't a part of my life beforehand, changed my daily routine (I don't own a personal scooter nowadays. I simply hop on a shared e-scooter from the "nest" near my house).

As part of the hush-hush work plan for building the company in Tel Aviv, I recruited some of my good friends. They helped ease the loneliness of being the GM in one country that is part of a much larger global start-up. We held business meetings and dealt with fateful questions like pricing[5] and team building on Omer's (my talented friend who wrote the intro to this book) living room couch. Omer recommended I bring in Nadav "Naji" Einav, a friend from our Midburn camp – a driven young guy who had just finished his engineering degree – to be our "on the ground" guy, who would be responsible for all things vehicle related.

I couldn't believe my eyes when, in the middle of that first job interview with Patrick on a hotel rooftop, Naji

---

5. The rate we chose was around five Israeli shekels to activate the service (about $1.40 at the time) and then about 50 agurot (100 agurot = 1 shekel) for about 15 minutes of use (or about a penny per minute).

casually lit a cigarette. But Patrick wasn't flustered. He trusted my judgment, and Nadav ended up becoming BIRD's second employee in Israel. Today, he serves as the branch's Operations Manager. He was sent to Rotterdam to learn more about the job before officially signing the contract. I continued searching for new people through friends, which was how I reached Dana Turbowicz, a lawyer looking to get into hi-tech. Like Naji, I promised her the idea of becoming part of the founding team. And similarly, she took the risk and became the company's third employee, working as the Senior Operations Associate, right after it launched. The two are still happy with their decision to step up to the challenge at just the right time.

As we recruited people, we rented a warehouse, as well as a manufacturing space, and I busied myself with developing the business strategy. At the time, the Beijing-based bicycle-sharing company Ofo wrapped up its activity in Israel earlier than expected. Its GM in Israel, Imri Galai, one of the stars on Israel's first Forbes 30 Under 30 list, offered to rent me the warehouse they were using, but we soon found out that the area was closing down due to renovations. Desperate for a place, we closed a deal for a warehouse on a street that wasn't really tailored to our needs. We'll get to it later. And as for Imri, the revolving doors of life worked well for him. The closing down of Ofo brought about the next big thing: he took his entire team and launched Wolt in Israel.

In my search for a good public relations manager to accompany BIRD's launch in Israel, I came across Yaniv Leibovitz, who previously worked with the successful company "Gett Taxi" (the Uber of Israel). After a good talk with him, I got the impression he'd be a loyal partner for the ride. At times, it's better to work with one person rather than a large PR company, where you're just one of many clients, and may get lost in the masses. During Patrick's visit to Israel, we met with Noa Tishbi, who fell in love with BIRD while in L.A., and she arranged a quick meeting with Tel Aviv's mayor, Ron Huldai. At that point, I was still holding on to the "fake it 'till you make it" motto and gave the mayor an impressive presentation where I mentioned the world's previous transition from horse-led carriages to cars. This brought me to the next big transition – a parking spot for 15 shared scooters instead of space wasted on one car. What seemed like science fiction at the time, a year later became reality, but at this stage, Huldai didn't want to commit to anything.

Again, it was my friends who came to the rescue and helped connect me with Rom Tene, then the chairman of Tel Aviv University's student union, who was extremely enthusiastic about the idea of shared e-scooters. Tene wanted them to operate around the university and be available to students. For me, it was a way to present this new venture as a collaboration with the student union on private land and not a fully blown launch in the city. After the collab, I informed the company's headquarters that we were set to go. BIRD's competing company, Lime, announced its launch in Paris, and thus it was decided that in August of that year, BIRD's first two global markets would open – on the 1st of August 2018, in Paris, and on the 14th of August 2018, in Tel Aviv.

The office in Amsterdam sent a launch team to help, and while our local team worked on fitting all the scooters in the warehouse with the operating system, I found the right contractor to handle their upkeep and repair. Collecting the scooters, as well as charging them, is done using a shared economy method in keeping with the company's ideology and is entrusted to the hands of "birdwatchers" – people (who aren't employees of the company) who collect the scooters when they're no longer in use, charge them at their homes, and return them in the morning to their "nests." They're rewarded based on the number of scooters they charged.

It was the call for "birdwatchers" we posted on Facebook that unveiled BIRD before its official launch. The tech website "GeekTime" was sharp enough to spot it, and on the 24th of July that year posted an article titled: "Is the Uber of Scooters on Its Way to Israel?" "A mysterious call on Facebook hints to the upcoming rental scooter trend that has taken America by storm," the article mentioned. "Its economic model allows users to earn money in an original way."

The post caught us off guard, but it only added to the buzz that accompanied BIRD from the day it was founded.

***

On the night between the 13th and 14th of August, I could barely get any sleep. So many questions flooded my mind: will residents of Tel Aviv fall in love with these shared e-scooters and use them? What happens if

Tel Aviv bans them? What are the chances of them getting stolen?

On the day of the launch, 50 e-scooters were scattered around the city, mainly around the central district and the university. If we would have expanded to other areas, the municipality might have grown suspicious and banned them. In addition, the fact that they were only a few peppered along the streets sparked interest. The demand for Birds and the search for them created a buzz, even frustration, and possibly encouraged people to buy their own private ones. All things considered – we acted wisely. I'm convinced that if we would have flooded the city with scooters, Tel Aviv would have confiscated them and banned the service to this day.

At 6 a.m., I headed out on my daily run with Ofir, tired and anxious, but seeing the scooters near the beach put a smile on my face. I spent most of that day gazing at a dashboard that provided information about the locations of scooters around the city, as well as following what the media had to say about them. I learned to let go over time, but on the 14th of August 2018, I let myself feel as enthusiastic and nervous as possible, for better or worse. I also appeared extremely excited in the interview I gave as part of an eight-minute piece broadcast on the day of the launch on Israel's main news channel. Despite all of my rehearsals, I didn't do very well. It was evident how nervous I was, as I occasionally stammered, especially when confronted with questions about authorizations from Tel Aviv's municipality. After the interview aired, the municipality released its response. "BIRD is requested to remove its scooters from any urban space."

This, of course, put me under a lot of stress, and we worked behind the scenes to solve the problem. It was impossible to imagine that, less than a year later, things would look completely different.

Travis stated from the start that we weren't going to market BIRD – the best commercial was the scooter on the street and the riding experience. And indeed, from day one, it was hard to ignore the e-scooters zooming around public spaces quite fast, maybe even faster than expected. They had quickly become an inseparable part of the landscape. It was impossible to remain indifferent. BIRD was the first company to confront society with the question of micro-mobility – commuting with small devices. Everyone had an opinion on the matter – users, pedestrians, drivers, journalists and legislators. Most of the marketing was done for us by the media itself. In 2019, a few months after BIRD launched, a major financial newspaper in Israel listed the shared scooters as one of the 100 forces to change the face of Israel. This is what it wrote:

"The scooter, a board with two wheels, the private transportation device taking big cities by storm, may remind you of our old scooters, as it is small and light as well, but it can reach a speed of 15.5 mph. There's no other device that provides that amount of speed and flexibility, demanding nearly no effort from the driver.

Cars and motorcycles require a license. Electric bikes are heavy. Scooters, however, give drivers the chance to cruise the streets like motorcycles, and hop on bicycle routes and sidewalks, illegally yet extremely common, all this without any regulatory barrier or any significant financial barrier. Using it via shared apps is the cheapest option for getting around big cities... the scooter is the first means of transportation to give Israel and its local authorities smart, shared, and available transportation. It's here to stay."

BIRD was a hit in Tel Aviv from day one. However, naturally, the success brought several challenges along as well. The first scooters weren't manufactured by BIRD – they were manufactured by Xiomi (we first had to test whether there was any demand for them), type M365, the most popular one bought by private owners. For that reason, they weren't really suitable for shared use, as shared e-scooters are stronger and sturdier due to the long rides and many users compared to private scooters. It took a while to learn what was needed for a shared e-scooter, one that wouldn't break easily. Only a year after we launched in Tel Aviv – after we proved a consistent level of demand, established the market we started from scratch, and raised further funds – did we hold a press party and launch the B1, a scooter that was specifically tailored and manufactured to meet our customers' needs, sturdier and with a larger battery. To understand the magnitude of BIRD's impact in Israel, I'll mention that Tel Aviv's deputy mayor herself, Meital Lehavi, gave a speech during that press conference.

Additional labor pains came in the form of theft, vandalism, and stolen batteries. We were prepared for those kinds of things to happen before the e-scooters would become a normal part of the city's landscape. Today, there's barely any theft, but about four months after we launched, I had to make one of the hardest decisions as the company's GM: we canceled the service in socio-economically challenged south Tel Aviv and placed scooters strictly in the city's central and northern districts. I had no choice. The amount of theft and vandalism in the south was significantly higher than in other parts of Tel Aviv, and we couldn't keep up with the rate of damage. We removed our service for several months – in complete contrast with my conscience and agenda, as I believe this service should be accessible for all – so we could stabilize ourselves. Of course, we were heavily criticized for this move – the stronger a brand is, the more fire it attracts – but with this level of vandalism, I couldn't convince the global team to keep providing services in that area. Even though those were tough times, the decision I made was inevitable, and in retrospect, I wouldn't have done it any differently. A few months later, we restored the services in the south of the city.

Another criticism fired our way pertained to safety. The more the scooters took off, the more backlash we received about users' crazy use of them on sidewalks, an issue that existed beforehand, but this time, we were the address for the complaint. One of Israel's leading papers, Globes, turned it into their central focus and released a daily list of the number of victims hurt by scooters. Naturally, the more scooters that were used in the city – a good thing in and of itself, as it decreases the number of cars – the more people that were injured as a result. Statistically, we saw a rise in the number of scooter users. Any means of transportation, scooters included, will bring about accidents, and unfortunately, at times, fatal ones. The tragedy of one of Israel's famous movie directors, Avi Nesher, whose son died after being hit by a car as he rode an e-bike, made headlines, and it tremendously affected industry regulations.

In the beginning, we contributed to events stressing the importance of safety measures. We handed out helmets, added safety remarks to our apps, and held safety workshops in partnership with an Israeli NGO. Further along, as the topic became more popular, I appeared before the Knesset (Israeli parliament) committees dealing with the issue. Nowadays, not only is wearing a helmet mandatory, but BIRD itself now has to equip its scooters with helmets. A new market requires education and the cultivation of new habits, and the fact that today fewer scooters are seen strewn randomly by the side of the road speaks for itself.

The work was challenging and intense. In October, two months after the company launched, my heart sank when city inspectors entered our offices, served me a warrant, and demanded we remove all scooters from the city due to illegal use of public spaces. The scooters weren't removed, and the order was never complied with. Stephen Schnell, BIRD's former Chief Operating Officer once told me: "We invented this field, and we ourselves don't have it all figured out yet."

The fact that we were the first ones, in the world and in Israel, to step into a yet unconquered territory gave way to both innovation and entrepreneurship as well as setbacks and challenges. The beauty was in the process. We kept learning as we went, constantly testing what was right and what was wrong, learning by trial and error. Each day, we were faced with new questions – pricing, taking care of the scooters, and tending to birdwatchers. We learned something new each day.

One of my biggest advantages was that I'd lived six years in North America working at an American foundation, so I knew how to speak to an American audience, as well as how to mediate for Israel in America (and as the brand grew, I learned how to speak 'European' as well). A global perspective means not only viewing your country from the outside but understanding its nuances and both the major and minor differences between cultures.

For example: In the U.S., it's customary for an applicant for a certain position to send a thank you letter after their job interview. In fact, certain companies will disqualify applicants for not sending one. In Israel, this doesn't exist.

The first incident predicated on cultural gaps happened during the first week of launch at a seemingly minor event that had little to do with the work itself. As part of the onboarding of new employees, the company's headquarters looks to deepen their acquaintance with new people by asking them personal questions, for example, asking them to point out their favorite song. And when one of the answers given by one of the employees was sent to the company, Patrick called me and said the words that every leader dreads: "We have a problem." As it turns out, that employee's favorite song had the "N" word in it. The company considered firing the person, but I refused to let her go. I went all the way to Steve Schnell to convince him that she was a terrific person, and a great employee, and if her choice of song raised some eyebrows, it was only because of an innocent, cultural gap. On that call, which was also with the head of HR, I even threatened to quit. Good leaders need to back up their employees and fight for them, especially when they deserve it. To my delight, but not without consequences, Patrick and I succeeded.

Additional cultural gaps were noted on a sweltering day in August when the production team came to Israel and were appalled to see that the storage facility we rented wasn't exactly fit for our needs, and certainly didn't meet American standards. The path leading down to the storage facility was terribly narrow, and on that scorching hot morning, a truck loaded with scooters got stuck midway. As stubborn Israelis who don't give up and can always come up with creative improvisations, we rolled up our sleeves and unloaded the scooters ourselves. The American production director slipped a curse word under his breath, and I believe also muttered something about "these people" who were supposed to be running a business operation. However, I managed to mediate the situation with the Americans so that they'd see the positive side to this predicament: the beauty of Israelis is that, while we're not always organized, we're great at coming up with improvisational solutions.

The fact that I managed to survive this event amicably doesn't mean that I didn't write a note to myself on where to improve. The job of a leader is to always check up on things, from top to bottom. Never freeze in place, and never take anything for granted. It's important to adjust and modify things on time. Ask yourself whether you're in a good place and if the answer is no – change things up. I knew that the storage facility on that narrow excuse of a street wasn't fit for the company, and yet, we held on to it for several months, even when we knew we needed a new one. I ended up fixing this problem (albeit belatedly), and we finally moved to a far more suitable storage facility in a different area.

In November 2018, "Wind," our first competitor, landed in Israel, and in February 2019, came "Lime," our biggest competitor yet. Of course, competitors rising to the scene brings with it a host of concerns, but at the end of the day, competition makes you better. First, it's clear evidence that you must be doing something right and that the market is responding positively to your idea. Second, it keeps you on your feet, alert, and doesn't allow you to rest on your laurels. Also: in a new field, from a regulatory perspective, it's always better to have a few players in the game. Initially, I was the only one representing the benefits of shared e-scooters. Today, several other people share my interest and help push this field forward.

Bottom line, BIRD, being the first of its kind in Israel, is the most commonly known name in the market, just like the iPhone is people's default when thinking of mobile phones because it was the first one to arrive. With all due respect to our competitors (which we have), BIRD is, undoubtedly, the shared e-scooter.

***

Toward the end of our first year, during which Tel Aviv's municipality mainly stood on the sidelines and observed the developments, it decided to join in on the fun as well. There was no arguing our success: in a city of 480,000 residents, the number of rides completed was around 2 million, with 250,000 unique users! A year later, the numbers skyrocketed to 5.5 million rides and 350,000 users (Tel Aviv is among the top-five most successful markets among the company's 400 cities around the world). The municipality concluded that e-scooters were the best, most efficient solution in reducing the number of private cars on the city streets and turning Tel Aviv into a much greener city. Moreover: the data collected by the company and transferred to the municipality – accurate information based on ride monitoring – was unprecedented. This information helped the municipality make smart decisions about the public sphere, like where to expand bicycle trails and where to place bus stations. With the help of this technology, city hall could also lay out regulatory rules concerning e-scooters, for example, banning them from specific areas. We also complied with their request to limit the scooter's speed to 15 km per hour in crowded areas. BIRD, on its end, managed to truly revolutionize Tel Aviv. A dream and a vision became a reality. Parking lots were scrapped for e-scooter "nests" – something that truly felt like science fiction materializing before us. As part of a program promoting cycling and micro-mobility, Tel Aviv set a goal for itself: to increase the number of rides using micro-mobility vehicles in the city by the year 2025 to 22% from 7% today. At the launch of the program, Tel Aviv's deputy mayor said that many of the bicycle paths were paved thanks to the information that BIRD passed on to the municipality and praised the company for its real and significant impact in the public sphere. In the municipality's video about the expected transportation revolution of the city, when discussing forms of shared commuting, the presenter rode a BIRD scooter. There was no better proof than that for the change we had made – and the evidence kept pouring in, and our collaborations kept growing.

BIRD's buzz in Israel consistently grew, and two months after launching, I participated in an annual financial forum. Despite my fervent preparation, I botched my speech somewhat, but have improved greatly since. Practice makes improvement.

In December 2018, Wall Street Journal reporter Jason Singer came to Israel to write a piece on artificial meat. When he saw the scooters whizzing around the streets, he called his editor to tell him about this micro-mobility revolution in Israel and convinced him that it was worth a story. At that stage, one out of every three Tel Avivians had ridden a BIRD scooter. In the interview with me, shot on a pleasant winter day at the beach, Singer began with these words: "It's December, and life in Tel Aviv is a beach." This was a great achievement. After Singer, several other major outlets dropped by, including Bloomberg, AP and Newsweek. The revolution was as clear as daylight.

I discovered my love for sales in Canada, working at the mall, chasing after potential customers with Dead Sea products. Now, with far more experience but equally as passionate, curious, and ambitious as I was in the beginning, it was clear just how much I loved sales, which is an inseparable part of our lives. I sold the scooter to its users, municipalities, and press. I firmly believe that a leader should be connected with their product, and in BIRD's case, the connection was immediate. All along the way, I was committed to these life-changing scooters, and I enjoyed hearing feedback from its users (as well as complaints), and some were, in fact, surprised by how available and accessible I was as the GM. There's no better way to familiarize yourself with your product than to be out there in the field.

One of the things that stood in my favor, right from the beginning, was the fact that I was the company's first GM. While I didn't have someone else to learn from, I did have a lot of room for exploration, trial and error, and improvement. And when others came around, I had plenty of experience by then. I learned a lot from this period. Among other things, I learned that I truly enjoy and am suited to the broad job description of a GM, which is in line with my personality: having an array of skills, and not a specific specialization.

This collection of skills, along with the experience I had garnered, helped me deal with the mistakes made along the way. Luckily, none of these mistakes were colossal. However, I blame myself for missing out on an opportunity to break into another important city at a time that, for many reasons, was perfect for us (but we'll get to that later). While I strongly believe in building trust and delegating, I gave too much responsibility to a certain vendor, until their interests were no longer aligned with mine and, to a certain extent, I lost my ability to monitor them. The mistake was entirely mine.

I was also wrong about stressing over every little thing written about me or the company in the beginning. This is just how the world works, and how every young GM takes their first steps. Luckily, I have since then adapted to look at things from a much broader, more calculated perspective.

When Covid first interrupted our lives in March of 2020, two and half years after BIRD launched, I was ready to deal with the crisis, and I'm quite proud of how I did it. As the world began shutting down, I was asked to pause the service and remove all devices from the streets. However, I knew this wasn't the right way to go about it, certainly not in Israel, a sturdy country that has survived plenty of catastrophes. I asked them to let me keep going. Transportation is a vital service people rely on, and when it vanishes, scooters grow in demand. I knew that even if the number of rides decreased significantly, BIRD should still remain part of the city's social tapestry. My status in the company was established by then, so I was given enough leeway to do things my way, the only provision being that we remained cashflow positive.

While Lime had suspended its services, BIRD remained in the city and adjusted to the new reality – we decreased the number of scooters based on the demand and released several of our workforce on unpaid leave. We lost money during that time (though we were cash-flow-positive!), but our presence in the city and the message to our customers were no less important: the company remained part of the urban fabric, even in dire times. People thanked us for the opportunity to continue commuting when public transportation was kept at a minimum. In line with my vision of companies operating to make our world a better place, we also collaborated with an emergency medical service organization and allowed their drivers to use our scooters for free, expanding our work with them substantially during the first lockdown. We granted free rides for medical teams and volunteers who distributed food packages to those in need (in partnership with OneDay). We also branded some of our scooters at the time after partnering with Bumble, a feminist dating app. After all, the city was in need of an optimistic, romantic boost.

***

Three years after the first "birds" showed up in Tel Aviv, it was evident that the company had revolutionized the face of the city and, hopefully, would continue transforming transportation all around the country. The company has since expanded to other cities in Israel as well, along with rural areas, and the list is growing.

During the company's Christmas party in December 2019 in Amsterdam, Patrick walked into the lounge with my favorite song at that time, "High Hopes," playing in the background. Only a year and a half prior to that moment, it was just the two of us, Patrick and me. And now, at that party, we had 350 employees.

BIRD's success became, of course, my success as well. I was lucky enough to become the Israeli GM of one of the world's fastest growing companies, and since joining them, I was promoted three times in a span of three years. Most recently, I was promoted to regional GM and a director at the global company, turning me into a partner in the company's global decision-making process.

In September 2019, TheMarker, one of Israel's prestigious financial papers, included me in their "40 Under 40" list of Israel's most promising young leaders. A month later, I was recognized by Haaretz newspaper and Samsung with my friend and entrepreneur Adi Altschuler, as part of the ten most influential trailblazers in Israel. These incredible acknowledgments were important for my ego, but I could also feel that my stock was rising.. My name even ended up in gossip columns when I made public appearances at event launches. I'm not going to lie: the growing interest and fame was flattering.

Amid all the hard work and incessant chasing after success, one needs to know when to stop and smell the roses. Elon Musk once said that, at times, we treat our achievements as trivial, ones that others could have also achieved. Loyal to the advice of my professor, Ron Heifetz, to "take a step to the balcony," I know how important it is at times to lean back and observe things from the outside – including my achievements. They're not to be taken for granted.

My Word to the Wise

- Examine your weaknesses, go over things you need to learn, and figure out what's lacking in your portfolio so you can continue to develop.
- Build a team that will complement your shortcomings.
- At times, it's best to "fake it till you make it" – project confidence and tell your story in a way that frames everything you've done in a positive light, even if you know that you're lacking specific skills required for the job (assuming, of course, that you are certain you can do the job).
- Use your relationships to make the right connections between people – with discretion and wisdom. Successful connections are beneficial to you and others and cultivate good karma. Unsuccessful connections can harm others and tarnish your reputation.

A Word to the Wise from
ADI ALTSCHULER,
Founder of "Krembo Wings" and "Zikaron Basalon"

"Be the catalyst for change"

Don't ask anyone for permission. Worst case scenario, you might have to apologize.

Follow your heart, don't wait for others. Be the catalyst for change, right here and now, without fear. Who knows, you might even succeed.

Eleven years ago, I had forgotten that Holocaust Remembrance Day was to commence later that evening and was reminded thanks to a few sad songs playing on the radio. I didn't know what to do. Without many options, I ended up joining my mom at a ceremony at the Tel Aviv Culture Center. When I entered the auditorium, I scanned the audience and realized that I was the only one under the age of 60. Where was everyone? I wondered: What were people my age doing today? The ceremony opened with the lighting of torches by Holocaust survivors. I thought to myself that by the time I'd have children old enough to understand something about the world, there wouldn't be any more Holocaust survivors living among us.

The ceremony itself bored me; it was a classic Holocaust Remembrance Day gathering. I thought: *Why should we commemorate the Holocaust?* So many horrific events are happening in the world today, does anyone here know about them? And what will all this look like in 20-30 years? Will only a small fraction of society mark this day? On my way from the ceremony to the car, I heard voices coming from an adjacent building. I peeked into the living room of one of the apartments and saw a group of people huddled together, watching the UEFA Champions League. A soccer game.

Suddenly, it hit me: maybe the problem was, in fact, the solution. Maybe I didn't need a big ceremony, but rather, all I needed was a living room. Maybe, if I would've attended an intimate evening in a living room, maybe... instead of gathering in a large hall echoing the sounds of a ceremony someone else had worked on, I would have organized the event myself, and things would feel different? Instead of hearing about six million perished Jews, I would have heard the story of one person, either dead or alive, and the discourse would've connected memories from their past with our lives here in the present – turning someone else's history into a memory of my own.

A year later, my partner and I invited over twenty friends to an evening we called "*Zikaron Basalon*[6]." Forty people showed up, some of whom we had never met before. I invited a Holocaust survivor, Hannah Gofrit – a brave and wonderful woman – to share her story. During our chat beforehand, she told me: "A living room suits me far better. Big stages are too much for me." I asked two of my friends to prepare songs, and my partner to

---
6. Literally "memory in the living room" in Hebrew.

guide the discussion, which he opened with the question: "Why are we even here tonight?"

When Hannah sat down to talk with us, the first thing that came out of her mouth was: "I hope I won't disappoint you, because I wasn't at Auschwitz and I don't have a number tattooed on my arm. I was just a little girl who ran away. I hope my story will be good enough for you." In that very moment, everyone sitting in the living room went from pure strangers to one unit, one heart, beating together, intertwined by destiny, not fate. When Hannah shared her emotional and inspiring story, we felt like she was sharing not only her story with us but her DNA, our shared DNA. Similar to Passover dinner – when parents tell the tale of the Exodus from Egypt to their children, and then their children pass the same stories on to the next generation. And like the *Haggadah*, the book of the Passover *Seder*, we played the role of the child who doesn't know what to ask, but knows how to feel and experience, and longs for something other than national slogans. After we played music, sang songs, and had a meaningful conversation built on values and life lessons, I felt – for the first time in my life – that I managed to touch on the topic in a way that made me feel connected.

Another year passed, and whoever was in my living room last year, opened quite naturally, their own living rooms for a similar evening. There was no fixed protocol, and each gathering looked different. On Holocaust Remembrance Day in 2021, 1.5 million people attended "Memory in the Living Room" in 55 countries around the world. Individuals were taking responsibility for our collective memory, without anyone asking them to do so, without asking permission from anyone. These people are the ones ensuring that Holocaust Remembrance Day will remain alive and meaningful.

CHAPTER 10

Between Midburn and Times Square

So many things happened in the months after I finished writing the chapter you just read and when the Hebrew edition of this book was published in February 2022. As if all the lessons and insights I had learned crystallized into a compressed period of time, justifying their existence and proving themselves an integral part of my life on this never-ending journey. This phase had everything: highs and lows, deliberations and decisions, initiatives and fate, the ability to receive and give back, recognition and gratitude, passion and love. Lots of love.

***

Along with the success of BIRD, other tempting offers began to pile up. Loyal to the question guiding me every step of the way – do I have where to advance in my current state? – I knew that I still had a long way to go with BIRD, but there was another nagging question on my mind: how else could I enrich my resume? For that reason, when an offer popped up on LinkedIn from a "headhunter" in the summer of 2020, I didn't completely toss it aside. The offer: GM of Israel's Yango.

Yango belongs to the company Yandex, a huge Russian corporation working internationally across many fields – among them, transportation, media, search engines (the company founded the Russian versions of Facebook and Google), electronic trade, online marketing, and more. It's one of the biggest companies in the world, with a market cap of over $20 billion. While I didn't want the job, I didn't rule it out right away either. I wanted to take advantage of the proposal to understand my own financial worth in the market, because I felt that BIRD, being an American brand, didn't know how to financially adjust my pay in Israel and that I wasn't being appreciated enough in terms of compensation. I love this company, it's become part of my DNA, but this doesn't negate the importance of receiving fair pay.

My goal was to find the best offer and present it to BIRD.

After ten interviews with Yandex, including with the company's founder, I received an offer far greater than what BIRD was paying me.

Not only that: Yango, which hadn't succeeded in Israel, had a lot to offer me in terms of interest. I love challenges, and I had a lot of ideas on how to turn the company into a successful enterprise. I had an exciting opportunity to become part of a mother company far bigger than BIRD and learn about its many markets. On the other hand, I felt that at BIRD I was part of an unfolding revolution and that even after three years with them, my potential still hadn't been exhausted.

I thought about my current goal. I knew that if BIRD would meet Yandex's offer, I'd stay. Therefore, I didn't wrap things up immediately, but rather, used the subtle, American way of probing. I didn't shove the offer in BIRD's face, nor confront them aggressively – steps that instantly breed antagonism – but I presented them with the offer and told them that, in all honesty, I preferred to stay at BIRD and that the company had become part of my life's fabric. Yet, at the same time, I found it important to be valued and paid accordingly. I remembered the genius method that my friend, Libby, taught me, how to be amiable when talking with airlines to get luxurious compensation for small mishaps. It was the right strategy.

I was fleeing from Portugal (which had just turned "red") to Milan – traveling the world during a global pandemic called for strategic thinking – when I received the long-awaited phone call from BIRD. They told me how much they appreciated me, and ultimately, translated the appreciation into money: offering me shares of stock worth the difference in pay Yandex offered. I decided to accept their offer, even if it was risky, because I genuinely believe in the company.

I was happy to stay at BIRD, a decision I wholeheartedly stand behind. When I was debating between these two offers, I thought about what I'd want to talk about at the Friday dinner table, and the answer was clear. That being said, there's no denying that thoughts of "what if..." persisted. What if I would have agreed to Yandex's offer? Where would this lead me – this classic sense of FOMO (fear of missing out) is part of life. There's nothing wrong with it.

***

2021 was a fascinating year. Life raced forward like a heart-stopping roller coaster, pumping adrenaline through my blood. At the start of the year, I was assigned to manage BIRD's Government Relations Department in EMEA (Europe, the Middle East, and Africa) and I got a raise in salary and stock options. Taken together, the sum was higher than the offer I received from Yandex. The coveted role of Government Relations Director – precisely what I studied at Harvard – is usually a job for someone with 20 years of experience. Not many of my Harvard classmates had reached that position, and I, as well, had little chance of getting there if I hadn't been at the right place at the right time – joining the company from the very beginning – and if I hadn't steered it in the right direction in Israel. Choosing this path wasn't exactly standard, as start-ups are high-risk investments, but it proved successful. I gained the education I lacked in business without doing an MBA, or better put: I graduated with life's MBA.

Success came with a price. I found myself working three jobs – GM in Israel, regional GM in Europe, and Government Relations Department Director – certainly not an easy undertaking. Along with the two former jobs, which were already pretty demanding, I had to study a brand-new field in which I had no experience.

The stress crept up on me. The first two months on the job were a nightmare. I didn't know what to focus on. There were moments of sheer collapse, I was on the verge of panic and depression, stemming from the workload and thoughts of not being good enough. I felt like I was drowning. The last time I felt a similar feeling was at the start of my career with the Schusterman Foundation. Change is complicated, and one needs to know that, but at the same time, one needs to learn from the past and believe in oneself.

Oh, and in the midst of it all, I got married.

Eventually, things came together. With the help of my fantastic team, I overcame the initial crisis. Every day is another lesson learned in the school of life. And the wedding? A 30-hour festival celebrating our love on the shores of the Dead Sea. It was no less than perfect, thanks to my wife, Ofir, who took matters into her hands and created an unforgettable experience. Even the setback we faced along the way (the beach wasn't available on the original week we wanted to get married, the week we celebrated our engagement), was a blessing: that same week, all events were canceled due to a military operation in Gaza.

And then BIRD began preparing for its IPO (Initial Public Offering). The quickest unicorn company in history broke another record when it reached, four years after its formation and before all of its competitors, an IPO on the New York Stock Exchange. In other words, we fulfilled every start-up's dream. This is where the big money is and can be worth much more than the salary itself. The days prior to our trip to New York were tumultuous, a mix of professional and personal matters. On a personal level, I was dealing with my mom's recovery from another complex medical procedure. Toward the end of the week, on Thursday, we arranged an event encouraging women to hop on scooters, along with the minister of transportation, minister of environmental protection, and deputy mayor of Tel Aviv. Around 150 leading women, who wanted to take part in this revolution, participated in the event.

Transportation Minister Merav Michaeli delivered a dramatic announcement on stage when she said: "We are flipping the pyramid on its head" – no more roads will be paved in Israel. Instead, we will encourage the use of two-wheelers to ease congestion. Environmental Protection Minister Tamar Zandberg discussed the connection between the use of two-wheelers and efforts to reduce air pollution.

Despite all of these events, I didn't want to miss out on the Midburn Festival happening that same week. So, on Friday, I drove down to the desert with a small backpack. By noon I'd already changed into my Midburn outfit, which consisted of purple leggings and a cowboy hat, and set out for a 20-hour-long journey in the wondrous desert. I spent time with my friends from the camp, with whom I gathered for a lovely Friday dinner comprising 200 guests. Together, we sang and danced in celebration of Judaism, Israel, and community, right until the crack of dawn. On Saturday, at nine in the morning, I headed back, and by nightfall, I was on a plane.

After a 24-hour layover of hugs and kisses in Canada, at the home of my 92-year-old bubby Esther who couldn't make it to my wedding, I continued on to New York.

Alongside the company's founder, I stood proudly at the New York Stock Exchange – the world's financial Mecca, which was now plastered with BIRD's logo, where every MBA student dreams of standing one day – wearing a suit I hadn't worn in ages and holding on to a scooter. My heart thumped. As I sipped on champagne to the sound of the trading bell, I thought of my career path, and the decisions I had made along the way. I was lucky enough to become part of the micro-mobility revolution with a huge impact on what our world would look like far into the future, and lucky enough to stabilize myself financially. In the revolving doors of life, I managed to choose the right one.

***

Wait, this isn't the end. Something else happened that year, something no less important: I utilized my multidisciplinary skills, which allow me to think creatively and combine several disciplines, to help make the world a better place. Lynn Schusterman had always stated that she built her house in Jerusalem, overlooking the Old City, to serve as the center point of philanthropists looking to invest in Israel. At the time, when I carried out Reality trips, I used to do these "giving back" and "pay it forward" meetups with organizations relevant to the crowd I brought in from abroad, and I wanted to continue this work in my new job. I believe that giving back fosters good karma and multiplies itself effortlessly.

More than 16% of the unicorn companies in the world are Israeli, truly disproportionate to the size of our population. In 2020-2021, 9,000 new millionaires were added to the Israeli population. The tech community in Israel has received stock worth over $30 billion. Despite that, 65% of donations to Israeli organizations came from abroad at that time, and most of the donations in Israel, consisting of small sums, came from private households. In Israel, donations are just half of one percent of the national product. In the U.S., just to compare, we're talking about 2%. Those getting rich in Israel, most of them from hi-tech, don't always know how to give back to their society. Therefore, I want to give them the tools to do so. Making money is just one side of things. No less important is how you use it to make the world a better place.

For that reason, I decided to establish a philanthropy venture called "1point8," targeting all high-tech employees in Israel willing to donate 1.8% of their equity compensation. Every few months, the community will present impactful programs changing the face of Israeli society, and the fund will help to support that. Research has shown that presenting projects helps raise donations, not only in monetary terms, but also through the contribution of knowledge and skills of foundation members who feel more engaged and encouraged to lend their support. My friend, Assaf Harlap, a talented businessman who founded MEET (Middle East Entrepreneurs of Tomorrow), donated to the venture and connected me with the Keshet Foundation to manage the financial side of the project.

At that same time, I got to know Dr. Lior Zoref, an international TED speaker (if you haven't watched his speeches, you must!), an expert in crowdsourcing, and a social entrepreneur. He invited me to lecture at "Yesh Matzav," a non-profit he formed helping at-risk youth and those who suffer from "educational scars." The NGO does so with the help of one-on-one coaching and inspiring meetings with leading experts, who, as adolescents, managed to overcome hardships as well. As you have read in this book, I, too, have suffered from my fair share of "educational scars," so I was happy to talk to ninth graders and share my personal story.

Lior and I realized that we shared similar views on education. I deeply connected with the organization and its mission and was tremendously happy when Lior offered me to join its board and help it grow. Of course, I donated a generous amount to the NGO, and I'm truly excited to see how it will impact the country's youth. Lior, on his end, connected with the vision of my venture , "1point8," and volunteered to polish the projects presented on "demo days" to potential investors.

I also put Lior in touch with the commander of the elite Talpiot unit, who developed a new program for the unit in Katzrin to encourage youth to integrate into key technological positions, so that he would contribute his knowledge and experience. It was a converging moment between the shared vision of the three of us, and my starting point, my hometown. Everything connected at once.

***

So, what's next? Honestly, I don't have an answer to that question. If you would have asked me five years ago whether I'd create and spearhead the shared e-scooter sector, I probably would have laughed right in your face – precisely how I would have reacted if you would have told me 25 years ago that I'd be accepted into Harvard. What I do know, however, is that whatever I'll do, I'll ask myself the right questions beforehand, those same questions that led me to write this book.

I know this much about my next roles: they'll be about improving the face of society both in Israel and beyond, they'll be meaningful and challenging, and they'll wake me up each morning with a sense of joy and excitement for the day ahead. And even then, I'll be on the lookout for the next big thing.

***

I chose not to alter this book after it was first published in Hebrew, despite the changes that occurred in my life. I left BIRD and now head an investment fund for the advancement of Israel's periphery, and travel to speaking engagements across the globe. I lost my dad. And I became a dad! After all, the principles and insights that have always guided me haven't changed. All of this and more will wait patiently for the next book.

I'd love to hear from you:
Yanivrivlin1@gmail.com

Made in the USA
Middletown, DE
24 April 2024